# Teaching and Supporting
# English Learners
## A Guide to
# Welcoming and Engaging
# NEWCOMERS

Eugenia Mora-Flores, Ed.D.

Stephanie Dewing, Ph.D.

Foreword by Mary Hanson

## Publishing Credits

Corinne Burton, M.A.Ed., *President and Publisher*
Aubrie Nielsen, M.S.Ed., *EVP of Content Development*
Véronique Bos, M.S.Ed., *VP of Creative*
Cathy Hernandez, *Senior Content Manager*
Hillary Wolfe, M.A., *Developmental Editor*
David Slayton, *Assistant Editor*
Kevin Pham, *Graphic Designer*

## Image Credits

pp. 196, 197, 198 courtesy of Eugenia Mora-Flores; all other images Shutterstock and/or iStock

**Shell Education**

A division of Teacher Created Materials

5482 Argosy Avenue
Huntington Beach, CA 92649

**www.tcmpub.com/shell-education**

ISBN 978-1-0876-4886-6

© 2023 Shell Educational Publishing, Inc.

# Table of Contents

# Foreword

Imagine that you have moved to a new country where you do not know the language or understand the culture that you are immersed in. You are then expected to start school within days of your arrival and learn the grade-level content in this new language and compete academically with your native-English-speaking peers. This is the overwhelming reality that our newcomer students face upon their arrival into the United States.

Now consider being a teacher with 24 diverse students in your classroom, trying to meet the needs of this unique population. Where would you start? With the growing diversity in our schools today, teachers need additional tools and techniques to create inclusive classrooms that support all learners. When I began teaching newcomers twenty years ago in Colorado, there were no resources, textbooks, or teaching materials to support teachers in their work with newcomer students and their families. Often, I would be given the grade-level textbooks and told to teach my students both the content and the English language, as well as provide the social-emotional support required for our students transitioning to life in the United States. Not surprising, I continually felt inadequate, overwhelmed, and disheartened that I was not doing enough.

Today, we have curricular programs that provide general support and suggestions for teachers trying to meet the academic and linguistic needs of our multilingual students, but these guides are rarely sufficient for teachers to reach and teach our newcomer students to thrive in their academic settings. That is where *A Guide to Welcoming and Engaging*

*Newcomers* bridges the gap between our grade-level curriculum and the unique needs of our newcomer students. This book not only gives teachers a clear picture of who our newcomer students and families are, with the opportunity to hear the students' stories firsthand, it also provides strategies for family engagement and instruction that increases language input and output. Teachers and administrators will be able to take what they learn from this book and immediately integrate it into their classrooms and school communities.

Providing this instruction are Dr. Eugenia Mora-Flores and Dr. Stephanie Dewing, two experts in the field of teaching multilingual learners and faculty members at the University of Southern California (USC) Rossier School of Education. Their experiences range from teaching in K-12 dual language, bilingual, and newcomer programs, to extensive research and teaching on topics that include second language acquisition, Latino culture, literacy and academic language development, and integrated language development. This wealth of knowledge and experience has been gathered in this incredible resource to instruct and guide teachers in their work with our newcomer students and their families. Research and theory in the fields of Teaching English to Speakers of Other Languages (TESOL) and Bilingual Education (BE) provide the foundation for the engaging and applicable strategies and techniques shared within this text.

During my years of teaching newcomers at the middle and high school levels, I have learned just as much from my students and their families about their home languages, cultures, and traditions as I have taught them about English and academic content. Working with students who are brand new to the United States has been one of my greatest professional joys, and *A Guide to Welcoming and Engaging Newcomers* will provide all educators with the tools and resources to have a similar experience.

—Mary Hanson, M.A.
Instructor, Teaching and Learning
College of Education, University of Colorado, Colorado Springs

# About the Authors

**Eugenia Mora-Flores, Ed.D.**, is Assistant Dean of Teacher Education and Professor of Clinical Education at the Rossier School of Education at the University of Southern California (USC). Previously Chair of the Master of Arts in Teaching program at USC, Eugenia teaches courses on first and second language acquisition, Latino culture, and literacy development for elementary and secondary students. She leads doctoral students in a wide range of research in teacher education. She began her work in education over 25 years ago as a first-grade, dual-language teacher and went on to teach a range of grade levels and instructional contexts. Her research interests  include studies on effective practices in developing the language and literacy skills of English learners in grades Pre-K–12. She has written 10 books in the area of literacy and academic language development (ALD) for English learners, including *Connecting Content and Language for English Learners, Balanced Literacy for English Learners,* and *Inquiry-based Science for ELs*. She has also published a number of articles and chapters on literacy and language across the curriculum and on gifted education for ELs. Eugenia works as a consultant for a variety of elementary, middle, and high schools across the country in the areas of comprehensive literacy programs for English learners, English language development (ELD), ALD, and writing instruction. She was named *MAT Professor of the Year* (2016 and 2018), a title awarded by the students of USC. Eugenia was further honored with USC's *Teaching Excellence Award* (2018), the USC Rossier *Mentoring Award* (2021), and the 2022 *USC Mentoring Award.* Her impact in education was recognized through the 2018 *Community Achievement Award.* This award recognizes professors who have gone above and beyond for their students and who have made meaningful contributions to the education of students of color and/or who identify as LGBTQ.

**Stephanie Dewing, Ph.D.**, started her career in education in 1998 after graduating from the University of Illinois (U of I) with a degree in the teaching of Spanish. Her journey began in Quito, Ecuador, where she taught English and social studies at a K–12 bilingual school, and English as a second language (ESL) at a local university. Upon returning to the U.S., she went back to U of I and earned her M.A. in TESOL while teaching adult ESL in their intensive English program. Since then, she has taught ESL, Spanish, English language development, and Spanish heritage, and co-taught algebra at the secondary and post-secondary levels for many years. She

also worked with the Department of International Programs at the United States Air Force Academy. From there, she started a new path on her educational journey as a teacher educator working with both in-service and pre-service teachers on strategies for supporting their multilingual and English learners. She spent several years working with the M.A. TESOL program at the University of Colorado, Colorado Springs, during which time she earned her Ph.D. in educational leadership and innovation from the University of Colorado, Denver. In 2018, Stephanie joined the Rossier School of Education at the University of Southern California, where she is currently an Assistant Professor of Clinical Education and Chair of the Bilingual Authorization Advisory Board. She continues to support in-service and pre-service teachers across the country through coursework and professional development in the fields of language and literacy development and dual-language instruction, with a particular emphasis on newcomers. She lives with her husband and three children in Colorado Springs, Colorado.

# Acknowledgments

We would like to say a heartfelt thank you to the newcomers who shared their stories with us. Without you, this book would not be possible. Thank you for inspiring us and helping us continue to learn and grow. We would also like to thank the educators who shared their experiences and best practices for supporting newcomers in the classroom and beyond. Your insights were invaluable.

# Introduction

We started writing this book on our very first day of teaching. As teachers, we remember the many moments we shared with students, families, and colleagues who taught us what it means to listen and learn from others. Day to day, for over 25 years, we kept our ears, our minds, and our hearts open. There were days when we felt successful as teachers and other days when we struggled and could not figure out how to connect with and engage our learners. But these struggles taught us so much about ourselves as teachers and as partners in the education of our students. This book is a reflection and a celebration of our careers as teachers working alongside diverse student populations who enriched our lives with their stories and made us part of their educational journey.

We believe all students are learning and developing their language skills in diverse linguistic settings. Throughout the years, we have worked with a range of language learners. However, we focused our work on the education of students who were learning English as a new language in the United States. This population has been generally referred to as English learners (ELs), and over time has come to be seen as a group of language learners with some common needs but with unique histories and language experiences that inform how we teach them. We believe that these students should be encouraged not only to learn English but to continue to develop and celebrate their heritage language *and* to learn languages other than English.

While we believe that ELs are truly multilingual learners, we use the term *English learner* in this book to represent those multilingual learners who have been identified as needing additional support in English language development. When students enroll in school, their caregivers complete a home language survey that indicates whether a language other than English is spoken by the student or their family at home. Once a language other than English is identified, students are administered a language exam to determine their level of English language proficiency. Students who have a strong grasp of the English language are considered initially Fluent English Proficient and are not identified as needing additional support to develop English. Those students who do not demonstrate a certain level of proficiency are classified as ELs and provided additional support to guide their language, literacy, and content needs. In this book, we use the term *English learner* because in our scholarly and professional work as teachers we have focused on students who were identified as needing additional language support. This does not represent our comprehensive understanding and support of students' maintaining and developing their multiple languages. We advocate for all ELs to be supported as multilingual learners.

Over the last 15 years, advocates for the education of English learners have encouraged a more intentional asset-based approach to how we refer to these students, using *emerging bilinguals* and more recently *multilingual learners*. Using more diverse and inclusive language is important in showing support for individuality and for equity-minded approaches to teaching and learning. The California Department of Education (2020) released a comprehensive resource to guide the education of multilingual and English learners. This guide uses the term *multilingual learners* to represent the range of diverse students who are developing two or more languages. The document further explains how the term *English learner* is situated within the diverse group of multilingual learners (see figure I.1. below).

Figure I.1—Multilingual Learners

## Multilingual Learner Students

All students who are engaged in developing two or more languages

| Dual Language Learners<br><br>Children ages zero to five who use a language other than English in their home. | **English Learners**<br><br>Students in transitional kindergarten through grade 12 (TK–12) with a primary language other than English, whose English proficiency upon enrolling in school dictates a need for support to access instruction in English and develop English proficiency. |
| --- | --- |
| | **Initially Fluent English Proficient (IFEP) Students**<br><br>TK–12 students with a primary language other than English who demonstrate proficiency in English upon enrolling in school. |
| | **Reclassified Fluent English Proficient (RFEP) Students**<br><br>TK–12 students who were initially identified as English learners upon enrolling in school, but have since achieved English proficiency. |
| | **Native English Speakers Learning a Non-English Language**<br><br>TK–12 students who have never been identified as EL, IFEP, or RFEP, but who are developing proficiency in an additional language. |
| **Birth** → **Age 5** | **Transitional Kindergarten** → **Grade 12** |

(California Department of Education 2020. Used with permission.)

We chose to focus this book on the diverse newcomers who make up a group within the larger multilingual and English learner population. We have taught a broad range of ELs, written books about supporting all English learners, given presentations, and led professional development sessions focused on English learners. We ground our work around ELs in learning about them as individuals with a collective need for further language support. However, we understand that language needs are not the same for all English learners. Each group of ELs, across and within different typologies, has unique needs. These experiences were the inspiration for this book's focus on newcomers. We have worked closely with newcomers and felt that their stories are often blended within the larger EL population. We wanted to capture the diversity of the newcomer population. Many teachers and administrators told us about the growing populations of newcomers in their schools and the need for support with helping them. We heard from newcomers themselves about how they were struggling,

feeling that some of their teachers did not understand who they were and what they were going through. They struggled to learn English and keep up academically. These interactions with educators and students inspired us to tell their stories and ours to support this unique group of ELs. This book looks at newcomers, but we understand other groups of English learners deserve the same dedicated focus and we hope to share their stories and address their needs in future books.

## How This Book Is Organized

This book begins with a discussion of the diversity of the newcomer population and leads into hearing from a range of newcomers who were brave enough to tell us their stories. We ground our work in this book in those stories to help educators learn how to provide comprehensive language, literacy, and content support to maximize learning, including social-emotional support and family engagement strategies. The book is organized into nine chapters that move from learning about students and their families to instructional approaches to guide learning.

**Chapter 1**, "Who Are Our Newcomers?," introduces newcomers as a unique subset of the overall EL population. We review the identification and assessment processes, the different categories of newcomers, and demographics, such as percentages and top languages spoken. In addition, we share ideas for how to get to know your newcomers and ideas for how to foster their first-language development while simultaneously teaching English. We conclude with a discussion about the power of story.

In **Chapter 2**, we are honored to share the stories of 13 different newcomers who had the courage to tell us about their experiences. They represent five continents and range in age upon arrival from 3 to 17, preschool through high school. This chapter is the heart of this book. It is the students' voices that provide the greatest insights into how we can be most effective in supporting them. In each story, you will hear about the newcomer's background, journey, first time in the U.S., and school experiences. In addition, each newcomer shares their advice both for teachers working with newcomers and for other newcomers.

**Chapter 3** is dedicated to the social and emotional needs of newcomers. Even though their experiences are diverse, they have one thing in common—being new. They are new to the country, the culture, the language, and the school system. Before learning can happen, we must ensure that our students feel safe and have a sense of belonging. We provide multiple strategies in this chapter for how to accomplish that important goal.

Strategies for engaging newcomer families are presented in **Chapter 4.** Some newcomers come alone as unaccompanied minors. However, many come with family members. It is critical for schools and educators to extend their support beyond the student to include the family and/or caregivers. We share a variety of ways in which you can create a welcoming environment for newcomers' families, communicate in their preferred language, help them navigate the school system, and connect them with essential resources.

**Chapter 5** gives an overview of designated English language development. Providing newcomers with a time of day that is focused on instruction in the English language helps differentiate language needs for newcomers. Designated ELD meets students where they are in language. It provides instruction based on students' English development level and literacy needs, rather than being content or grade-level dependent.

In **Chapter 6** we explore integrated English language development, which is part of a comprehensive approach to supporting newcomers. We explore what it means to provide language support across the curriculum. All content-area teachers at all grade levels are teachers of language. But what does that mean? This chapter provides a framework that guides teachers in explicitly supporting newcomers as they access, comprehend, interpret, and produce language across content areas. We share questioning practices, language supports, and a guide for identifying the language opportunities within different content areas. In addition, we consider essential daily practices that can be used by all teachers to support teaching content through a focus on language.

**Chapter 7** pushes beyond daily practices shared in Chapter 6 to provide a wide range of language input strategies teachers can use to help students comprehend content and language when reading and listening. These strategies are intended to be used for specific purposes. All strategies shared in this chapter come from our work in classrooms as teachers and professional developers. They have been used in all grade levels and content areas.

Practicing language for a variety of purposes further supports language development. Language output strategies are the focus of **Chapter 8**, which reminds us that we cannot rely on students to simply understand language; they need opportunities to *use* language as well.

The content and strategies shared in this book are presented through the lens of working with newcomer English learners. However, we understand that many of the practices support all learners as they develop their language skills. We encourage teachers to take what they learn from this book and make it their own. Whether or not any strategy or instructional practice is a success depends on how well it meets the needs of the students in each individual classroom. We wrote this book to be a companion, a colleague that teachers can connect with to get ideas for improving and reflecting on their own practice. To support this, each chapter ends with reflective questions that guide teachers to celebrate their current practices and find ways to continue to improve their teaching for the language, literacy, and social-emotional development of their students.

# CHAPTER 1

# Who Are Our Newcomers?

As an educator, when you hear the term *newcomer*, what comes to mind? For us, we think of the many students we have worked with over the years who have enriched our lives in countless ways. We think of the young people who have taught us so much about diversity. We think about the countries, languages, cultures, religions, family dynamics, and education systems that they have helped us better understand. We are humbled by the struggles that they have endured and inspired by the resilience that they have shown. We vividly remember the stories they have shared with us about their journeys to the United States—some of which were extremely dangerous—in search of the "American dream" or a better life for their families.

## Definitions

A *newcomer* is defined as a person who has recently arrived in the United States from another country, typically within the past two years (U.S. Department of Education 2016). If they arrive from a country that does not have English as its official language, newcomers in the K–12 school system may also be identified as English learners. To determine this, districts typically request that during the registration process, families complete a home language survey that asks about the primary language spoken in the home, the language most often spoken by the student, and the language the student first acquired. If the family indicates that a language other than English is dominant in the home, the student is then given an assessment (e.g., WIDA Screener, Initial ELPAC, TX, ELPA 21) to determine their English

**WIDA**—WIDA stands for World-class Instructional Design and Assessment. The name WIDA originally stood for the three states on the grant proposal: Wisconsin, Delaware, and Arkansas. Today, it represents a community of member states, territories, federal agencies, and international schools. The organization developed the WIDA English Language Proficiency Standards, most recently revised in 2020, which serves as the basis for the ACCESS for ELLs test of English Language Proficiency. In addition, WIDA provides tools and resources to support multilingual learners, families, and educators.

**ELPAC**—the English Language Proficiency Assessments for California (ELPAC) is (at the time of this writing) the required test for English language proficiency (ELP) that must be given to students in California whose primary language is a language other than English.

language proficiency level. This data provides a starting point, but follow-up interviews provide additional pertinent information on their background and experiences.

Newcomers represent a unique population of K–12 students. They require special understanding, consideration, and support. To that end, this book strives to equip educators with practical and effective strategies that can be incorporated immediately to best support newcomers in the classroom and beyond. The practices presented in this book will be illustrated by the lived experiences of newcomers themselves who have shared their stories with us. They represent a wide range of ages, backgrounds, and experiences. We will introduce you to them in Chapter 2 and make explicit connections between their stories and the content throughout the book.

Who makes up our population of newcomers? Due to the fluid nature of immigration and migration, the demographics change and shift frequently. For example, following the withdrawal of U.S. troops from Afghanistan in 2021, and the Russian invasion of Ukraine in 2022, there was a great influx of refugees. Based on political and/or world events, natural disasters, and other factors, we see ebbs and flows of immigration trends. With that in mind, the statistics presented in figures 1.1–1.3 are simply snapshots in time highlighting the cultural and linguistic diversity of our most recent newcomer population. The data is drawn from research compiled from the Migration Policy Institute, the U.S. Census Bureau, and the U.S. Departments of Homeland Security and State.

Figure 1.1—2019 American Community Survey (ACS) Data

1 in 7 people in the United States are foreign-born
(about 44.9 million)

5.5 million foreign-born children over age three are enrolled in school

**Note:** The term *foreign-born* includes naturalized citizens, lawful permanent residents, refugees, asylees, people on certain temporary visas, and those who are undocumented.

(U.S. Census Bureau 2021)

Figure 1.2—Top 10 Countries of Origin

| Country of Origin | Approximate Percent of U.S. Immigrants in 2019 |
|---|---|
| Mexico | 24% |
| India | 6% |
| China (including Hong Kong and Macao) | 6% |
| Philippines | 5% |
| El Salvador | 3% |
| Vietnam | 3% |
| Cuba | 3% |
| Dominican Republic | 3% |
| Korea | 2% |
| Guatemala | 2% |

(Esterline and Batalova 2022)

The fastest growth over the last 10 years has been from Nepal, Venezuela, Afghanistan, Syria, and Nigeria. The expansive list of countries from which our newcomers arrive represents rich linguistic diversity as well. The Census Bureau reports that more than 350 languages are represented in the United States (Batalova and Zong 2016). Of course, language use varies across states and school districts. Nationally, Spanish is the most common language spoken in the United States after English, with approximately 76 percent of English learners speaking it (National Center for Education Statistics 2021).

Figure 1.3—Top Five Languages of English Learners

| Language | Percentage |
| --- | --- |
| Spanish | 75.7% |
| Arabic | 2.6% |
| Chinese | 2.0% |
| Vietnamese | 1.5% |
| Portuguese | 0.9% |

(National Center for Education Statistics 2021)

It is important to note that while in most cases newcomers' first language is something other than English, some come from countries whose official language is English, such as Jamaica, Nigeria, Belize, Singapore, and Tonga, to name a few. While not all newcomers are identified as English learners based on their home language survey results, we should still be ready to support their transitions into a new country, culture, and school system.

There are countless reasons why people come to the United States. Some of those reasons include fleeing war, gangs, persecution, human trafficking, or slavery in their home countries. In addition, many come to seek economic and educational opportunities, a "better life," or to reunite with relatives already living in the United States. Based on the unique circumstances of each student or family, *why* and *how* they come to the United States varies. Knowledge about a student's *why* and *how* can help us better understand the social-emotional factors we must consider, the support the student needs, and the resources available to them.

Several terms are used to describe newcomers based on their circumstances and reasons for coming to the United States, such as *immigrants* (documented and undocumented), *refugees, asylum seekers/ asylees, unaccompanied minors/youth*, and *international adoptees*. These terms are defined below. In addition, we will briefly discuss migrant students, students with limited or interrupted formal education, heritage speakers, and long-term English learners. While not all of these students are newcomers, many have similar linguistic support needs in the classroom. This list is not all-inclusive, but it considers the most common classifications to help us understand the *why* behind our students' reasons for coming here and the *how* of the journeys they took to get here.

## IMMIGRANTS (DOCUMENTED AND UNDOCUMENTED)

Merriam-Webster (2022b) defines an *immigrant* as a "person who comes to a country to take up permanent residence." Immigrants in the United States are usually referenced in one of two ways: documented or undocumented. For an immigrant to be considered documented, they need to obtain a "green card." Green cards, officially referred to as Permanent Residence Cards, allow immigrants to live and work permanently in the United States. There are several pathways for obtaining a green card: through family, employment, or refugee or asylee status; as a victim of human trafficking, crime, or abuse; from special circumstances; and other categories (United States Citizenship and Immigration Services [USCIS] 2020). Regardless of pathway, though, the process is often complicated and can take many years. For more information about the processes and procedures for establishing permanent residence in the U.S., see Resources, page 239.

Because of that lengthy and often arduous process, there are many immigrants who are living in the United States who are waiting to begin the process or who are living in the country without "green card status." They are considered undocumented, which means "without papers" (USCIS 2020). Undocumented immigrants often live in a state of uncertainty, isolation, and fear (Kaplan 2020). Some undocumented students arrived in the United States when they were very young, meaning the U.S. is the country they know as home. It is difficult to imagine the daily fear of being deported to a country you do not know and potentially to a place that speaks a language that you do not speak. Or even worse, carrying the unimaginable fear that your family could be separated. This is a real concern for many students who sit in our classrooms, which ultimately impacts their ability to focus and learn. While they may or may not have experienced trauma in their past, the emotional impact of being undocumented affects students' social-emotional stability and well-being.

> **affective filter**—a metaphor that describes a learner's attitudes that affect language learning. Negative emotions such as anxiety, fear, or embarrassment can hinder language learning.

Both documented and undocumented immigrants go through a process of adjustment, which is often stressful. Language development research has proven that when students are anxious, nervous, or stressed, their *affective filters* go up and can impede their ability to learn and develop language effectively (Krashen 1982). Recent brain research confirms this phenomenon (Hammond 2015). The takeaway for educators is that immediately after confirming that students' physiological needs (water, food, shelter) are met, we should be addressing their safety needs and feelings of love and belonging (Maslow 1943). (For more information about the social-emotional needs of newcomers, see Chapter 3.) Ultimately, one of the most important things we can do for newcomers—and all students for that matter—is to help them feel safe and cared for. Angela Valenzuela's seminal ethnographic study on immigrant and native-born Latino students found that "authentic care" that "emphasized relations of reciprocity between teachers and students" (1999, 61) was essential to students' academic success.

## REFUGEES

A *refugee* is a person who is "unable or unwilling to return to their country of origin owing to a well-founded fear of being persecuted for reasons of race, religion, nationality, membership of a particular social group, or political opinion" (U.S. Department of Homeland Security [USDHS] 2020). By the end of 2021, more than 89 million people worldwide had been forcibly displaced due to war, violence, conflict, or persecution (United Nations High Commissioner for Refugees 2022), which is an unimaginable number. The problems refugees face are severe and urgent. Despite this urgency, the process of refugee resettlement to the United States can be lengthy. Refugees are required to apply for Lawful Permanent Resident (green card) status within one year of arrival. It takes multiple agencies and several years to complete the process. This means that most refugees spend time in refugee camps—often years, sometimes decades—prior to coming to the U.S.

Figure 1.4—Top Ten Origins of Refugee Admissions, Fiscal Year 2021

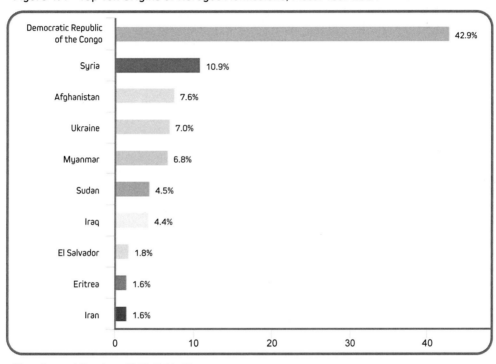

(Esterline and Batalova 2022, Table 5)

The countries named in figure 1.4 account for about 89 percent of the refugee admissions to the United States. The remaining 11 percent come from other or unknown countries. Regardless of country of origin, refugees are protected by international law and because of that, there are several organizations and agencies, both governmental and non-governmental, in place to support them. Some examples include Lutheran Family Services, Catholic Charities, Interfaith Refugee and Immigration Services, and International Rescue Committee, but they vary from state to state. We encourage you to find out about your refugee population and sponsors—qualified parents, guardians, relatives, or other adults to whom unaccompanied children are released; parents are preferred, followed by legal guardians, and then other adult family members

the local agencies in place to support them. You can search by state at: **acf. hhs.gov/orr/map/find-resources-and- contacts-your-state**. As with other newcomer populations, it is important to keep in mind that most refugees are fleeing danger and have likely experienced trauma, which will impact how they learn and interact with others. Getting support from local agencies will help refugee students and families experience success in the classroom and beyond.

"There are refugees who get invited to this country and they get officially placed through an agency. But we have a ton of U.S. asylees who walk across the border by themselves. And they literally just have a little paper in their pocket [listing] all people they know who live in the United States, and [agencies] just start calling all those numbers to see if anybody will take them. It is usually people that they know from their village or extended family, or it could be anybody that they know in the hopes that somebody will take them. Because if not, they get stuck at the border in the camps, and they will be sent back if they can't find anybody to sponsor them. We have one case where [the agency] called five or six families. And then finally, a family said okay, he can stay with us, but usually those families don't truly take ownership in that situation because they didn't invite the person. It can be very tricky."

—High School ELD Teacher

## ASYLUM SEEKERS/ASYLEES

An asylum seeker must meet the same criteria as a refugee (fleeing danger, persecution, or violence in their country of origin). However, while a refugee's resettlement is documented and coordinated outside of the United States, an asylum seeker is already in the United States or is seeking admission at a port of entry (USDHS 2020). When asylum seekers are granted asylum, they are referred to as *asylees*. Figure 1.5 shows the top countries of origin for people who were granted asylum in 2020.

Figure 1.5—Top Countries of Origin of Those Granted Asylum in 2020

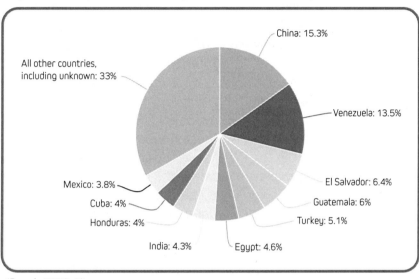

(Baugh 2022, 9)

Like refugees, asylees have likely experienced trauma in their country of origin. In addition, many have faced additional trauma due to the extreme dangers of their journey to get to the United States. Typically, students and/or their families who are in the process of seeking asylum must attend frequent court appointments, which often happen during the school day. Many of the same agencies that support refugees also support asylees (see the URL on page 16).

## UNACCOMPANIED YOUTH OR MINORS

Children under the age of 18 who come to the United States without their parents or legal guardians are often referred to as *unaccompanied youth* or *minors*. Unaccompanied minors come from all over the world. However, according to the Office of Refugee Resettlement (ORR), the vast majority come from Guatemala, Honduras, and El Salvador. Many are apprehended and detained at the U.S.-Mexico border (2021b). Once a child is confirmed to be unaccompanied, they are detained for up to 72 hours in a facility separate from adults. Exams, evaluations, and background checks are conducted, the child's rights are explained, and they are informed of free legal services. If the child is found to have a criminal record, they may be transferred to an alternate facility and possibly assigned a lawyer.

Many unaccompanied children meet conditions that make them eligible to remain in the U.S. legally. First, they can apply for asylum. Second, they can file for Special Immigrant Juvenile Status, which, according to the Migration Policy Institute, "is conferred upon immigrant children who can prove abandonment, neglect, or abuse and can lead to permanent settlement and, eventually, citizenship" (Levinson 2011). Or third, if appropriate, the child can apply for a T Visa, which protects victims of human trafficking. This is the least pursued option as most of those who would be eligible for T Visas are too afraid to come forward. Tragically, due to their age, circumstances, and often hazardous journeys, unaccompanied youth are especially vulnerable to human trafficking, exploitation, and abuse (Office of Refugee Resettlement 2021a).

The Office of Refugee Resettlement monitors and oversees these processes, which can take time and are often confusing and frightening for the children. Because the facilities used to house unaccompanied children were not designed to provide care for extended periods of time, they have been scrutinized for their poor conditions. While there have been some reports in recent years of improvements to the process, significant concerns still remain (Zak 2021).

"We have all forms of family separation [and it is] really, really tough. One of our kids walked over here by herself, and she had to leave her son. So she has a one-year-old at home who wasn't able to come to the United States with her. There's ongoing trauma with these kids and again, communication helps a lot. Sometimes it helps to just have somebody to talk to."

—High School ELD Teacher

As with other groups of newcomers, there are implications for educators when working with unaccompanied youth and supporting their social-emotional well-being. (See Chapter 3, page 69, and Resources, page 239, for information on how to help.) The trauma of their circumstances and journeys can lead to intense emotions and feelings of fear and insecurity. They have left home, family, and everything familiar behind. In addition, most of them departed due to traumatic life experiences. The journey to get to the United States is often dangerous. And then, once they are here, they are detained and processed, which is an overwhelming experience, especially for a child.

The uncertainty of what will happen next often exacerbates those fears and insecurities. Some unaccompanied minors are reunited with family members who came to the United States years prior. In several of those cases, the residing family members are, in essence, strangers to the child. This can lead to challenging and uncomfortable family dynamics. The alternatives are that the minor may be placed with families that they do not know or in group homes or facilities. Some end up without housing.

> "Our newcomer population is unique in that they all are unaccompanied minors. So, it's not like in some other school districts where you get the whole family system with mom and dad and the kids. Our kids come on their own and then they go into foster homes, which adds a layer that we have to work with because that's pretty hard on the student, as you can imagine, being not only in a foreign country but having left your family behind."
>
> —District ELD Coordinator

## INTERNATIONAL ADOPTEES

Students who have been adopted from countries outside of the United States are referred to as *international adoptees*. This group of students is unique since they may be living in English-speaking homes but have influences from other languages and cultures in their lives. That level of influence will vary based on the age at which the child was adopted and brought to the United States as well as their lived experiences in their home country prior to being adopted.

It is important to consider that the home language surveys that are completed by the families of international adoptees may indicate that they speak English only. However, schools should note that while English may be the dominant language spoken in the home, the child may benefit from English language development services if they learned and/or spoke a language other than English prior to their arrival.

## MIGRANT STUDENTS

Merriam-Webster (2022c) defines a *migrant* as "a person who moves regularly in order to find work especially in harvesting crops." Migrant students are typically children of migrant workers who move back and forth between states or countries of residence. The length of stay in each location varies and could last between three and 12 months or longer. The duration varies based on factors influencing migration, many of which are agricultural in nature. While not all migrant students move back and forth internationally, some do. Nationally, data suggests that approximately 90 percent of migrant children are of Latino origin, about 34 percent of whom are identified as English learners (Lundy-Ponce 2010). Frequent geographical movement leads to inconsistency in education in general and with language development and instruction specifically. Of particular concern with migrant youth is that graduation rates are lower and drop-out rates are higher (Lundy-Ponce 2010). Educators should be aware of a student's migratory status, educational experiences, and dominant language of instruction and interaction during periods when they are away from your classroom.

## STUDENTS WITH LIMITED AND/OR INTERRUPTED FORMAL EDUCATION (SLIFE)

Many refugees, asylees, and unaccompanied immigrant and migrant youth have gaps in their formal education. These interruptions are due to migration, time in refugee camps, journeys to come to the United States, and so forth. In some cases, students may come from places of residence that prohibited full access to formal education. While the circumstances vary from student to student, it is critical to identify those potential gaps to be able to address them.

## HERITAGE LANGUAGE SPEAKERS

People are often surprised to learn that the majority of students who are designated as English learners were born in the United States (Batalova and Zong 2016). Students who are born in the United States and who speak

> **heritage language**—also known as first language or L1, this is a language spoken in the home that is different from the dominant language used in academic or social settings

languages other than English at home are often referred to as heritage language speakers. While they are not newcomers to the country, they often require extra language support. For some, school will be the first time they are introduced to English. And unless they are enrolled in a bilingual program, they will likely receive English language development services.

## LONG-TERM ENGLISH LEARNERS (LTELS)

A student who has been enrolled in U.S. schools for more than six years, is not progressing toward English proficiency (based on state assessments), and who is struggling academically due to their limited English skills is referred to as a long-term English learner, or LTEL (Olsen 2014). LTELs may or may not have been newcomers at one point, but they do have unique circumstances and needs. While LTELs embody a host of cultural and linguistic assets, some become unmotivated or disengaged as a result of the extended periods of time they have been designated as English learners, received ELD services, and been unable to reclassify. In essence, they get "stuck" in the system.

# Getting to Know Our Learners

To best support our students, first we must get to know them. What is the newcomer and English learner population like in your district, school, and classroom? Start your initial search on your school's website or data platform (e.g., PowerSchool, Alpine) to find out which students are identified as ELs. If you are not sure where to find that information, talk to a school or district administrator who oversees ELD and/or multilingual programs. This should yield information about which students are identified as ELs and their most recent English language proficiency levels. From there, you can start the process of inquiry with the students themselves. This can be done orally or via surveys or journals, personal narratives/stories, bilingual poems, and more (see below for specific strategies). Understand that the students may not speak English yet, so it may be necessary to get creative with translation tools, bilingual colleagues or friends, and bilingual dictionaries, as well as pointing, using gestures, and providing visuals. Here are a few questions to consider for gathering information over time:

- Where are you from?
- Which language(s) do you speak?
- Why and how did you come to the U.S.? How do you feel about being here?
- What was your life like in your home country?
- If you attended school elsewhere, what was that like? If you worked, what was that like?
- What is your family situation like (e.g., who do you live with)?
- What are your cultural traditions?
- What are your religious beliefs and customs?
- What are your interests?

The answers to these and other related questions combine to form students' *funds of knowledge*, a concept that is described by Gonzalez, Moll, and Amanti (2005) as the knowledge and skills acquired by life experiences. The process of learning about students' and their families' funds of knowledge will take time, and everyone will have a different level of comfort with sharing personal information. Creating a safe, welcoming, and supportive environment is an excellent way to foster trust, which often leads to a greater willingness to share and personally connect. In addition, a bit of curiosity, resourcefulness, and creativity will go a long way. Below are a few examples of classroom-based activities to get you started.

## Personal Interest Surveys, "All About Me" Activities, or Picture Boards

Learn more about your students by asking them to complete a survey or "all about me" activity. For the youngest learners and newcomers who are new to their journey towards English proficiency, it may require creativity to find ways for them to share information that does not rely on words. One example is a picture board (draw/show a picture of your favorite food, animal, sport). Google Translate™ and Google Images™ are also helpful in achieving this goal.

## Personal Narratives and "Our Stories" Books

Ask students to write personal narratives both to get to know them and to support their literacy development. Specifically, ask them to tell their stories of coming to the United States, if they are comfortable doing so. Allow them to write in their first language if they have not yet developed enough English. Then, use a translation app or tool to help you read what they wrote. As they develop more English, they can *translanguage*, or use both languages to communicate, and eventually, write their stories fully in English. For a fun final project, compile the collection of stories with illustrations and pictures and publish them in a book. Figure 1.6 is an example from a sixth-grade student in Colorado.

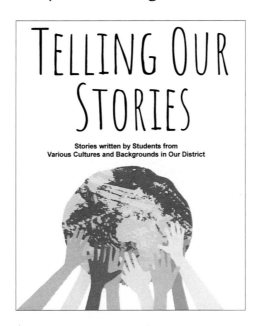

Figure 1.6—Sample Pages from an "Our Stories" Book

## My Journey to America
### by Sergey

**Motivation for Migration**

1. What do you know about your family's story?

We lived in Belarus.

2. Why did your family choose to come to this country instead of somewhere else?

My mother said that in America I will achieve more.

3. What did your family hope for in their new life here?

Good work.

**The Journey**

1. What members of the family made the journey and who stayed behind?

I, my sister, my grandad, and my mum go to America. My dad with my granny stay in Belarus.

2. Did anyone come ahead of the family?

My Aunt with my Uncle.

3. What was the most difficult for the family about leaving?

My dad, my cat, and granny stay in Belarus.

4. What was the journey to this new country (or community) like?

We fly on plane.

5. What does the family talk about having most surprised them when they first arrived?

Mountains.

6. What does the family talk about having missed the most about the country they left behind?

My dad, my grandma, and my cat stay home.

7. Who was the most helpful with getting your family settled in?

My dad and my mum.

Figure 1.6—Sample Pages from an "Our Stories" Book (Continued)

8. Migration can be hard. From where did your family gain strength in difficult times?

My aunt and my uncle help.

9. How do you think your family was changed by migration?

We happy here.

10. What was the most difficult for the family about arriving?

Missing my dad, my grandma, and my cat.

### Hope and Realities

1. How do you think the family's experience compared to their expectations?

I don't know.

2. What have been your family's biggest challenges?

It is sad that my dad and grandma and cat stay home.

3. What have been your family's biggest sources of joy?

We have a new cat.

4. Overall, how do you think your family is doing after your migration?

My dad help my grandma.

5. Can you think of times when your family has felt unwelcome because they are immigrants?

No.

6. What do you think were the family's hopes and dreams for the future?

Me and my sister get a good education.

7. In what ways do you think your family's migration has made you a stronger person?

Here we next to my aunt and uncle.

### Advice

1. If someone you knew were planning on coming to this country, what advice would you give them?

Ok, let's go!

## Dialogue Journals

Providing multiple low-stakes writing opportunities such as dialogue journals fosters literacy development and creates ways for you to get to know students and for them to get to know you. In a dialogue journal, students write a short entry on a given prompt (e.g., what you did over the weekend) or on a topic of their choice (e.g., favorite foods). Ideally this would happen daily or weekly. At the end of the week, they leave the journal with the teacher. Then, the teacher writes back to them and keeps the dialogue going. This is a great way to connect on a personal level. Students of all ages enjoy getting written responses from their teachers. Keeping in mind that newcomers will vary in their English language and literacy abilities, it is appropriate to allow students to write in their home languages and/or use bilingual dictionaries or translation tools as needed. If you do not speak or read their language, you, too, can reference online translation tools. Or, let them write without responding at first. Then, as they are able, encourage them to write the words they know in English. Little by little, you will be conversing fully in English. For those who have not developed literacy yet, substitute words with visual journal entries, such as pictures or emojis.

## Infographics

One fun activity to incorporate as you learn about students' countries of origin is to create an infographic. This hands-on, creative activity can be done individually or collaboratively. In addition to sending an inclusive message, it also supports students' geographical and cultural understanding. Include the name of the country, where it is located on the map, the country's flag, the main language(s) spoken, and other characteristics such as the population of the country, the breakdown of top religion(s), facts about the education system, and so on (see figure 1.7 for an example). The infographic is visually appealing and can be posted in the classroom and shared with others in the building. Hang copies of the infographic in the teachers' lounge or in the main office. Doing so shows that the school is welcoming and celebrates the diversity of the student body. This also helps other students and staff learn more about the newcomers in the school. Programs such as Canva®, Piktochart™, and others provide templates to get you started.

Figure 1.7—Infographic Example

## Group Google Map

Honor the countries of origin of students and help others learn a bit about their countries by creating a shared map using Google My Maps™. Put a "pin" on the location of each city/country represented in your classroom. Depending on the students' ages, help them do this or have them do it themselves. Link that pin to visuals, videos, or slide presentations. Find more information on how to create a map at **support.google.com/mymaps/.**

## Language Boards/Posters

In addition to learning about newcomers' countries of origin, learning a few key phrases in their first languages can foster greater communication with students and families. Design a bulletin board or a poster with those key phrases, and display it in the classroom or the main office to create a welcoming environment and show that you value linguistic diversity. There are multiple benefits to learning additional languages, so this is an excellent opportunity to engage in this powerful endeavor as a school community. To learn more than those few key phrases, there are a variety of options available. Local libraries often have programs and resources for learning languages. There are also online options, including free apps such as Duolingo® and paid programs such as Babbel® and Rosetta Stone®. (See Resources on page 239.)

## Group Diversity Calendar

Knowing the holidays, traditions, and other important events that students celebrate will help you honor their cultures and diverse backgrounds. Look online for Diversity Holiday Calendars (see Resources, page 239). These highlight important celebrations around the world. Turn this into a community-building activity by creating a shared calendar. Ask students and their family members to mark the important days that they celebrate throughout the year. This can be done either on paper or online through a shared Google document.

In addition to getting to know our learners as people, it is also important to learn about their home language, literacy, and academic backgrounds. Research tells us that early literacy experiences in one's first language provide a foundation upon which to build language and literacy skills in the second or additional language (Riches and Genesee 2006). Encouraging students to maintain their first language and build literacy in that language will give them advantages academically, socially, emotionally, and, potentially, financially. On page 30 are a few ideas to consider for fostering heritage language literacy development (adapted from Peregoy and Boyle 2017).

## Heritage Language Journals

Encourage students to write in a journal daily or weekly in their heritage language. These can be low-stakes writing activities with simple prompts that foster literacy (see Dialogue Journals above for ideas). Literacy skills developed in the home language will transfer to the development of literacy in English.

## Heritage Language Books and Backpacks

Add books in students' heritage languages to your classroom (or school) library. Put together "literacy backpacks" that students can take home and explore with their families. Check your local library or do an internet search to find bilingual books in your students' home languages. Here is one site that has a variety of books representing cultural and linguistic diversity to get you started: **colorincolorado.org/books-authors/books-kids**.

## Digital Resources

Keep a list of age-appropriate multilingual eBooks, magazines, newspapers, novels, or poetry in your students' heritage languages to share with them. Encourage students to find something compelling to hook their interest and continue reading to develop literacy. Audiobooks are a great option because students can hear how the language sounds and see it written simultaneously, which scaffolds language and literacy development. For example, "Cool Salsa" edited by Lori M. Carlson is available at **colorincolorado.org/booklist/poems-everyone**. For more examples, see Resources, page 239.

Students' prior content knowledge should also be taken into account. It is important to not make assumptions about their knowledge and abilities just because they may not be able to demonstrate that knowledge with words in English—*yet*. In fact, the education many newcomers received in their home countries was more advanced than what is being covered in their classes in the United States. Language development theorists such as Jim Cummins (as cited in Peregoy and Boyle 2017) have shown that content knowledge acquired in the heritage language transfers over and becomes available for use in subsequent languages learned, which is referred to as *common underlying proficiency*. This allows us to tap into students' prior learning to support their grade-level content and language development in English. In the end, the more we know about those prior experiences, the better we will be able to support students' academic progress and success.

As we engage in the process of getting to know our learners, finding ways to connect with them is a critical piece of the puzzle. We are hard-wired for social connection (Hammond 2015). As educators, caring about our students and making sure they know we care lays the foundation for more positive school experiences. (For more specific social-emotional considerations, see Chapter 3.) Here are a few ways to start the process of making connections.

- Ask them questions, even if they are not able to verbalize their responses in English *yet*. See the Getting to Know Our Learners strategies (page 21) and Adding *Yet* (page 31).
- Use translation tools, pictures, and gestures/body language to express interest and demonstrate caring.
- Find personal points of connection to relate to them (e.g., love of soccer, music, family traditions).
- Introduce them to buddies or other students who can help them with the transition and navigation of their new language, culture, and school system.

Each newcomer's experience is unique. As Chimamanda Ngozi Adichie (2009) reminds us, there can be "danger in a single story," and we need to be careful not to assume what our students and their families have been through based on their country of origin or status. However, while it is important to acknowledge the heterogeneity of the newcomer students' lived experiences, the ideas and strategies presented in this book draw on the commonalities of the newcomer experience in U.S. schools with respect to language and literacy development and the need for support in navigating a new culture and school system.

# The Power of Story

Research tells us that our brains are "wired for stories" (Hammond 2015, 135). As humans, we connect through stories, and we learn through stories. Getting to know our students' stories will foster deeper connections and understanding. In addition, knowing those stories can change how we see, understand, connect with, and teach our students. Stories are the mirrors through which we can see ourselves reflected as well as the windows through which we can better understand others' perspectives.

We had the great pleasure of interviewing current and former newcomers who shared their stories with us. We also interviewed teachers and administrators who work with newcomers, and they shared valuable insights based on what they have found to be most effective in supporting newcomers inside and outside the classroom. This collection of stories sheds light on the diversity of newcomers' circumstances and experiences. The voices represented are from all over the world and span multiple grade levels. The stories are centered around key themes of upbringing in their home country, their journeys to the United States, those first experiences in the U.S.—including school experiences—and finally advice to teachers and advice to other newcomers. Within their stories, you will hear about what it was like for them to make friends, navigate the U.S. school system, and get involved outside of school. Their stories start in the next chapter, and will be referenced throughout the remaining chapters as specific strategies are introduced, to highlight how real students are impacted by the efforts made by teachers and schools. These students also share things that teachers did, or things they wish they had done, to make their transitions easier.

# Adding *Yet*

As we share these incredible stories of challenge, triumph, and resilience, we want to express the importance of maintaining a growth mindset (Dweck 2013). For example, if we reference a student who does not speak English, we add *yet* to the end of the statement. We will teach them.

They will learn. When discussing the lack of friends that a child has as a new arrival, we are confident that they *will* make friends; therefore, they do not have friends—*yet*. When one particular refugee student does not understand how the drinking fountains work on the first day of school, add *yet*, because we will teach them how and they will get it. Adding *yet* represents the growth mindset, encourages us to hold high expectations for students, and holds us accountable for scaffolding their learning and experiences so they can successfully meet those high expectations.

## Summary

There is no denying the fact that newcomers and their families face a variety of challenges, as you will read about in their stories in the next chapter. However, we can make a difference. The common theme that comes across strongly throughout all the stories is the power and importance of relationships. As we get to know them, we will be better equipped to use their vast funds of knowledge as sources of strength and hopefully shift some of those challenges into successes. The information, tools, and strategies presented in this book will add to your own funds of knowledge and can be used as a guide for how to build upon the foundation of newcomer experiences to foster growth, language development, and success in the classroom and beyond.

## Reflection Questions

- How do you find out about the newcomers in your class or at your school?
- Which resources are available in your community that support newcomers and their families?
- What is the benefit of understanding newcomers' backgrounds?

# CHAPTER 2

# Newcomer Stories

We have spent the last 25 years getting to know students, their families, and their teachers. Throughout the years, we have come to learn their stories, their histories, and their experiences. We were humbled by their struggles and celebrated their successes. We are thankful that some of our students and families have offered to share their stories to help us and others learn from their experiences and guide us in our work in supporting teachers to meet the needs of this diverse group of English learners.

In this chapter, you will read about the adventures, successes, and challenges of 13 newcomers from five different continents. When they arrived in the U.S., their ages were between 3 and 17 years old, and their grades were from preschool to high school. They reflect on their journeys, initial feelings upon arrival, first days of school, making friends, and learning English. They share their advice and words of encouragement to other newcomers and those who teach them. These are their stories, their voices. Based on what they shared with us, we were able to extract a variety of effective strategies for supporting them, and all newcomers, in the classroom and beyond. Their voices will be revisited in the forthcoming chapters as they underscore the value of these strategies, by explaining what effective teaching means to each of them.

# CRISTINA

"You count, you belong, you are a person, you have rights ..."

| | |
|---|---|
| Age Upon Arrival:<br>**15** | Country of Origin:<br>**Colombia** |
| Grade Upon Arrival:<br>**8th grade** | Home Language:<br>**Spanish** |

## Background

Cristina was born in Bogota, the capital of Colombia, but grew up in a small town about four hours from the capital. Her father moved to the United States shortly after she was born. He moved back to Colombia when she was four years old but had another family and spent most of his time with them. Even though he was responsible for her financially, she only saw him occasionally. Her parents separated when she was nine years old. Cristina lived most of her life with just her mother and siblings. She described her mom as a strong, independent woman

who worked hard in the political world as mayor of their town, but who was also there for her children. Unfortunately, as her mom got more deeply involved in politics, their family started receiving threats. Cristina shared how "things got out of hand with the government" and "the guerillas were out of control." The continued threats and fear for her children's lives led to Cristina's mother's decision to leave Colombia for the United States.

## The Journey

When it came time to leave Colombia, Cristina, her mom, and her siblings flew to Miami. From there, they went their separate ways. Cristina's mom and siblings continued onward to Colorado. And Cristina, who had just completed eighth grade in Colombia, flew by herself to Boston to live with her dad. The look on Cristina's face that day will be forever etched in her mother's mind. It was a look of fear and surprise that her mom was leaving her at the airport in a new country without knowing the language. To say it was overwhelming is an understatement.

## First Time in the United States

Once she arrived, the mix of emotions continued. Even though she had finished eighth grade in Colombia, Cristina was placed in eighth grade in Massachusetts. She remembers getting all of her vaccinations and enrolling in the school system. It was a tough and uncertain time. "Most people didn't know about our culture," she shared. There were a lot of students from Puerto Rico and El Salvador, but not many from Colombia at that time. In fact, due to the cultural differences, or "clashes" as she put it, some of the girls at her new school thought Cristina was rude. She did not mean to come across that way. Even so, they threatened to punch and kick her. It was a scary and intimidating experience for Cristina and she did not feel safe in her new surroundings. As a self-described "outsider," she did not even grasp what was happening. Even though she was coming from war in Colombia, she had not experienced "war" in school until she arrived in the U.S.

## School Experiences

After nine months in Boston, she headed to Colorado to be with her mom and siblings for Christmas and ended up staying. She transferred to a high school there at age 16. It was hard for Cristina to start over again at another new school in the United States. These were some of "the most difficult times" in her life. There were moments when she felt "completely lost in translation and completely lost in the system" as she was just starting to learn English.

Reflecting on her most difficult and challenging experiences now, Cristina is grateful for the opportunity and for the teachers who believed in her, supported her, cared for her, and saw her. They made the difference for her—

> Reflecting on her most difficult and challenging experiences now, Cristina is grateful for the opportunity and for the teachers who believed in her, supported her, cared for her, and saw her. They made the difference for her—academically, socially, and emotionally.

academically, socially, and emotionally. Academically, teachers made her interested and engaged in the content, which helped her learn. Language and biology were her favorite subjects. Reading books and speaking with other students helped her learn English. Socially, having teachers get her involved right away made a world of difference. She was connected with a local mentoring group, became president of the diversity club, and learned to ski, all because of the encouragement of her teachers. Emotionally, Cristina indicated that she would have benefitted from school counseling because of all that she had to "deal with" in Colombia and her transition to the United States. Unfortunately, though, she said, "I never knew that I had a counselor until the end [of high school]. The real support was from my teachers."

## Advice to Teachers

Throughout her story, Cristina emphasized the important role that her teachers and other key adults in school (e.g., bilingual paraprofessionals) played in her transition to this new country, new culture, and new language. She described many of her teachers as her "go-to people." There were some, though, that were not. "They didn't impact me as much," she said. "I didn't interact with them as much. I feel like the language [barrier] for them was a big deal. . . . They just kept on with their lecture, which wasn't that impactful." The interactions, genuine caring, and language considerations she needed were not present in those particular classes.

As for social-emotional support, it is unfortunate that Cristina did not even know she had a counselor at school until it was too late. The system failed her in that respect. Cristina and her mom did end up seeking counseling outside of school, but finding someone who spoke Spanish was extremely difficult. This is an issue facing many schools, students, and families across the United States. We need to help our newcomers navigate the system and do our best to find available resources in their preferred language to get them the support they need.

Cristina's concluding advice to those working with newcomers is to make sure they do not feel alone and that they know there is "always going to be someone who will be there, who will listen and have compassion. . . . Provide a space where they feel welcome and safe; a space where they can be who they are and be accepted. Be there for them—no matter what. It is also important to do things together. Instead of saying, 'Go check this out,' or 'Go read this paper,' say, 'Let's check this out together. I'll go with you,' or 'Let's read through this together.'"

## Advice to Other Newcomers

Being undocumented upon arrival, dealing with the fear of seeing a police officer on the street or filling out forms for school, was a constant challenge for Cristina. Even something as simple as a field trip presented an obstacle and heightened her anxiety. These are deep fears that many of our newcomers face. She wants others who are undocumented to know that "you count, you belong, you are a person, you have rights." She wants them to know they are not alone, that this is their home, and that they are people just like everyone else and should be treated as such. Regardless of status, though, she encourages all newcomers to "hang in there. . . . It's one of those things that you have to experience and be okay with that struggle, knowing that someday, things will be different. It is going to be okay."

# AARON AND EVA (SIBLINGS)

*"I didn't like that I was outside of everything. I just wanted to be like everybody else."*

| Ages Upon Arrival: | Country of Origin: |
|---|---|
| **Aaron, 14; Eva, 11** | **Israel** |
| Grades Upon Arrival: | Home Language: |
| **Aaron, 8th grade; Eva, 6th grade** | **Hebrew** |

## Background

Aaron and Eva are a brother and sister who were born in Israel. Aaron was 14 and Eva was 11 when they left Israel and came to the United States. They arrived in Colorado and joined eighth and sixth grades, respectively. They grew up speaking Hebrew and continue to speak Hebrew at home with their family.

## The Journey

Their father's work as an electrical engineer initially brought them to this country on a visa; plus, there was "the really good education," as Aaron put it. "We thought we were going to move here just for a little bit and then go back. So we started out with just a normal visa and then we really liked it here. So we decided to apply for a green card and we got a green card now."

Eva described her brother as "very outgoing" and herself as "shy," especially when she was younger. She felt nervous when she first came to the United States. In particular, she worried about whether her English was good enough. Aaron admitted to feeling a bit nervous, too, but also excited—likely due to his more outgoing nature. He saw this as an "opportunity to learn English" and to learn about a "new and different culture."

## First Time in the United States

When they first started school in the U.S., they had mixed emotions. Since they did not initially plan to stay long-term, they felt it was more "like a trip" to start. However, after the first few weeks, things seemed to pick up speed.

Eva was "very scared" on the first day of sixth grade because everything was "shocking" and new—a new language, new experiences, a new school system. Sixth grade was her time to "catch up," because she felt the school in the United States was ahead of her school back in Israel. Even though she felt as though the people around her were "super understanding," that did not change the fact that the U.S. school system was very different from her school experiences in Israel. She particularly remembers her very first test. "I freaked out because I had never taken a test in my life! It was scary." Fortunately, though, her teachers were there to help her.

Making friends and feeling a sense of belonging were struggles at the beginning for both Aaron and Eva. That need for connection is human nature. They were used to being surrounded by friends back home and suddenly they were in a new school and had to start over. Eva shared, "I just remember really wanting to talk to people, but I didn't really know English, so it was really hard. You know what you want to say, but you can't." Aaron added similar reactions looking back on those first school experiences. "None of my teachers or students spoke Hebrew. It was frustrating because I couldn't speak to anybody. The only thing I wished in the beginning was to have a normal conversation with people, but I can't." He remembers only being able to communicate with people by "pointing to things and [using] Google Translate." Fortunately, though, he described people as "friendly and nice." And since the majority of our communication is nonverbal, those gestures and kindness helped ease that transition.

## School Experiences

When reminiscing about those first days and weeks, both Aaron and Eva emphasized the importance of their teachers who supported them inside and outside of the classroom. Eva explained, "The teachers did a lot for me and I know for my brother, too. They really did a lot that helped us." Aaron said his English teacher in particular went above and beyond for them. She made sure that they knew how everything worked. She even called them on snow days to make sure they understood the process since there were no snow days in Israel.

Aaron described her and the way she taught as "the best." Largely due to that system of support and encouragement, he was happy to report that over time, he started to "pick up the language," which increased his confidence.

> Beyond the safe zone of her English class, Eva expressed how important it was for her to have accommodations in all of her classes. Having a dictionary or translator and extra time were particularly helpful.

Beyond the safe zone of her English class, Eva expressed how important it was for her to have accommodations in all of her classes. Having a dictionary or translator and extra time were particularly helpful. Something that stood out to her was that while there were times when she had to advocate for herself, her English teacher also advocated for her and let other teachers know about the accommodations that she needed. That support stretched across her school experiences and impacted her overall academic success.

In addition to that support in school, getting involved in activities such as sports, clubs, art classes, speech and debate team, and more, helped them gain confidence, make friends, and learn English. Much of this was a direct result of encouragement from their teachers.

## Advice to Teachers

Aaron acknowledged that a teacher's job is very difficult, but patience and understanding are the most important things when working with newcomers. Some students, especially those who are learning English, might need to go a little more slowly. They might need more time or need instructions repeated a few times or information explained in a different way. He also stressed the importance of vocabulary and helping them learn as much vocabulary as possible.

Eva agreed. "I think time is the most important thing. And also encouragement." She admitted to lacking confidence in the beginning because she focused on what she did not know, which she believes is the case for many newcomers. However, teachers who told her she was doing well, and who convinced her that she knew more than she thought, boosted that confidence. Eva spoke fondly of a math teacher who, despite her almost giving up and being convinced that she was not good at math, helped her catch up and gain confidence. Eva started to think, "Maybe math is my thing." She thought, "There's no way I'll be in honors, and he was the one who suggested it. If he didn't suggest it to me, I wouldn't have done it. I didn't know if I was good enough to be in those classes but he put it on the table and [said], 'You should do it.' And I'm glad I did." Newcomers need teachers to believe in them, even when they do not believe in themselves (yet!).

## Advice to Other Newcomers

Eva's advice to other newcomers would be not to worry. "You learn way more than you think every single day." Don't stress about what you don't know, because "it will just come to you." It all comes in time—the language, the friends, knowing how things work. "Your brain is such a powerful thing and you will be fine." With respect to learning English, she suggests newcomers watch a lot of TV. She chuckled and said it was "kind of cheesy," but she really believes that watching *SpongeBob SquarePants* helped her learn English. She watched a lot of *SpongeBob* in Israel that was in Hebrew, so she understood the context, which helped her when she switched over to watching it in English. "You can see what's on the screen so you can kind of imagine what's going on. Even if you don't know a certain word, if you watch it long enough, then that's when you start learning about new vocabulary that you didn't even know."

Aaron encourages other newcomers to stay positive. While his initial lack of ability to communicate with others was negative, it had a positive end result. He hopes other newcomers view their experience as a unique challenge and opportunity that not many other people go through, which in the end, will make you stronger. You will learn life lessons that you can carry with you forever. "It changed the way I think about everything." You are special and that is an advantage in life. "People will see you as different and it's really good to be different. People that are different are usually the most memorable."

# MARIAMA AND BABACAR

"Sometimes you feel left out and you miss your home; you miss your friends. So that one's a little bit hard for us."

| | |
|---|---|
| Ages Upon Arrival:<br>**Mariama, 15; Babacar, 17** | Country of Origin:<br>**Senegal** |
| Grades Upon Arrival:<br>**Mariama, 9th grade;<br>Babacar, 10th grade** | Home Languages:<br>**Mariama—Fulani, Wolof, French;<br>Babacar—Wolof, Pular, French** |

## Background

While Mariama and Babacar are not biologically related, their stories are connected. They were both born and raised in Senegal, a country on the western coast of Africa. Their fathers were the first in their families to come to the United States from Senegal. And they both ended up in the same newcomer class in Colorado.

Babacar described growing up in Senegal as "great." He was born in the capital city, Dakar, but moved to a village in the northern part of the country when he was five years old. He lived with extended family, which is "how life is" living in the village—being raised to "value the importance of family." Babacar's father was living in the United States before Babacar was born. His father was born in Mauritania, and after the war between Senegal and Mauritania broke out in the 1990s, he traveled all along the west coast of Africa to Cameroon and eventually came to the United States as a refugee. Babacar remembers his dad coming back to visit them every couple of years. When Babacar was in middle school and starting high school, he became involved in clubs and other extracurricular activities and started getting involved in politics, which his parents did not like. He shared, "We would organize strikes—not go to school—go to the school door and tell students not to go in." They were advocating and fighting for a better education. There were not enough teachers in the school to support the kind of education Babacar felt they needed and deserved. This was "part of the reason why [I] was brought to the U.S." The other reason was because of the June 2014 mayoral election. "Things didn't go as we expected," he said. "[From] June of 2014 to May of 2015 we were basically marching against the mayor and all the projects the mayor had." Babacar described the election system as corrupt, which is why they were protesting. Ultimately, these circumstances led to his family deciding it was time to leave. Babacar actually thought he was going to be sent to France or Canada, which are Francophone countries, but "surprise, surprise," he said, he was being sent to "America." He admitted he didn't want to leave at that time, but it was "a one-time opportunity to live with my whole family."

Mariama's father was also the first one in her family to come to the United States. He came for job opportunities because, as she put it, even those with degrees still struggled to get jobs in Senegal. His initial journey was back in 1998, before Mariama was born. He could not get papers at that time, so he went back home. He returned to the United States in 2001 and reapplied. It was not until 2012, though, that he was granted citizenship. Then the rest of the family applied for papers, got accepted, and moved to Colorado a few years later, in 2015. During that time, Mariama lived with her mom and her four siblings: one brother and three sisters. She has another sister who was born in the United States. Mariama shared that she "actually never thought about coming to the United States," but like Babacar, her whole family wanted to be together.

## The Journey

Babacar and Mariama each encountered their first language barrier on their journey to the United States. When Mariama and her family arrived at the airport in New York, she remembered that they could not find anyone who spoke their language or even anyone to translate. Even though she studied a little bit of English prior to her arrival, she didn't feel confident with it. Because she knew a little, the responsibility fell on her to figure out what was going on. Once they got settled in, she said that people were nice, so "everything was okay." The importance of kindness, patience, and understanding cannot be understated.

Babacar's experiences were similar. He described arriving in New York as "crazy." He was traveling alone and remembered visiting three different offices in the airport in order to track down his luggage before boarding his final flight to Colorado. "I would write in French and they would write in English and use Google Translate. People were very helpful and finally, I got here on time." His dad picked him up at the airport. He remembers the day he arrived it was raining and it was also during Ramadan, which is a holy month during which time Muslims fast from sunrise to sunset. And while everything was "surprising," the large Senegalese community where they lived helped him adjust to the "new normal." His mom and sister joined them a year later.

## First Time in the United States

When it came time to start school in the United States, Mariama recalled the challenges of being a newcomer. "I was scared. I was [thinking], this is going to be hard. Especially when you don't have any friends at school and you can't talk to anyone."

For Babacar, it was similar. "It was frightening for a moment," he said. "But it was basically my only option. I just knew I had to finish school." He admitted that he preferred sleeping in to attending English classes in Senegal because his English teacher there did not even know his name, which made him unmotivated to attend. "I basically knew no English at all." He grew up speaking Wolof, which was the primary language in Dakar, and Pular, which is his parents' language, and then learned French in school. He remembers taking the initial English proficiency test when he arrived at school in the United States. He tried to use his knowledge of French to help him. "I was just trying to cheat my way out of it," he admitted, "but I barely knew five words in English." He felt as though his previous experiences with language helped him overcome some of that fear. "I was kind of used to being forced to learn new languages, to be able to adapt." In addition, having his teachers and some other friends from Senegal created a "small, safe community" which made those initial experiences a little less "scary."

## School Experiences

Mariama agreed that having friends like Babacar and a few others in her English classes made it easier over time, and more fun. She enjoyed playing games and being in a place where it was okay to make mistakes. The positive and safe environment was "the best ever," she said. There were other classes, though, that caused her to struggle, like health class. Things moved fast, and without any paraprofessionals or others there to support her and other newcomers, she felt as if they were on their own, which was tough. Both Mariama and Babacar expressed their appreciation for the classes in which they did have paraprofessionals who supported them.

Beyond the comfort zone of their English class, they found additional opportunities to grow and thrive. They both enrolled in the pre-collegiate program where they found new connections, systems of support, and a pathway to their future. In fact, Mariama's greatest memory of high school was graduation because she was the first in her family to graduate.

Babacar took a French class "just for fun." He enjoyed this class, in particular, because he got to be the expert. "It was my territory in a certain way," he said. "I guess that was fun. . . . It was helpful to be in an environment where, for one hour, I was kind of like 'home' whereas everybody else was struggling as I would be outside of the class. . . . That kind of took me 'home' for a moment—feeling safe in that environment." This experience not only helped his classmates develop a greater sense of empathy and understanding for what it is like to struggle to learn a new language, but it also gave him an opportunity to meet and socialize with people outside of his English class.

## Advice to Teachers

Both Mariama and Babacar highlighted the successes and challenges of being a newcomer in the United States. Creating that safe and welcoming environment, giving time and support where needed, genuinely caring, fostering a growth mindset, and having a little fun are the pieces of advice we can take from their stories. There were a couple of things they felt would have helped them even more. Babacar said that "going out more" would have been helpful. Teachers could "take students to Starbucks or something to see how they order. Or maybe grocery stores—stuff like that—things that apply to everyday life; getting them used to it and then building their confidence and

Mariama noted it would have helped if all of her teachers took the time to get to know her better. She wished her teachers knew that English was not her first language.

knowing that they have what it takes to be able to do those everyday things." Mariama noted it would have helped if all of her teachers took the time to get to know her better. She wished her teachers knew that English was not her first language. She also wished that teachers would not ask students to choose their own partners but rather choose partners for them. Choosing your own partner when you do not know anyone or the language caused extreme anxiety for Mariama. It is important to consider these small classroom logistics and how they might impact newcomers.

## Advice to Other Newcomers

Looking back and reflecting on the experiences of being a newcomer, Mariama encourages other newcomers not to be afraid. "When you come to the U.S., it's a different experience, which is great. So don't be afraid. You can do it." Babacar's advice to other newcomers is "to really give it their all because it pays at the end." He expressed that it is helpful to know there is light at the end of the tunnel and you can come out stronger on the other side. "Once you know that people have done that, it kind of gives you hope and the energy to put in the work that's needed . . . when you know that it is something that is not impossible. It's something that everyone can do. It's just a matter of putting in the time and energy necessary to do it."

# CASANDRA

*"I wish I had that support. I wish they knew that I needed help in my personal life. . . and I wish they had asked, 'Are you okay?'"*

| | |
|---|---|
| Age Upon Arrival: | Country of Origin: |
| **14** | **Guatemala** |
| Grade Upon Arrival: | Home Language: |
| **8th grade** | **Spanish** |

## Background

Casandra was born and raised in a small, rural town in Guatemala. She and her family lived on a farm and raised animals and crops such as tomatoes, potatoes, corn, and cabbage. "We planted that stuff to be able to survive," she shared. "We [would] sell them so we can have something to eat or to have something to buy clothing." She lived there with her mom, two brothers, and sister for 14 years before coming to the United States.

Casandra described her home country as "beautiful" and admitted that she misses it a lot. However, due to the economic hardships in Guatemala, it was difficult for people to get an education and strive for a "better life." Most of her classmates only finished elementary school. Some were fortunate enough to complete seventh or eighth grade, but many could not due to the cost of education. Casandra expressed gratitude for her father who helped change that for her. "I'm so thankful that my dad did everything and gave me everything to be able to come to this country and get a better education."

## The Journey

Her father came to the United States about 10 years before the rest of the family. After those 10 years, he applied for his green card. Once he was issued those documents, he applied for Casandra, her mom, and her sister. Her brothers went to the United States separately and on their own. When she was 14 years old, Casandra, her mom, and her sister joined them.

## First Time in the United States

Despite feelings of gratitude for her family's sacrifices to get her here, Casandra struggled with how different everything was when she first arrived in the United States. "Talking, the environment in school, all the stuff you eat, what you wear, going to school . . . it's all completely different. I experienced culture shock." During those first days, weeks, and months, she "cried a lot." The language barrier was a challenge for her. She felt "lost" and wondered what people were saying, where and when her classes were, and what they were about. Teachers assigned her homework and then asked her why she didn't complete it. She felt overwhelmed because she didn't understand what the expectations were and didn't have help outside of school since English was not her, or her family's, first language. School was not the same for her here as it was in Guatemala, and the adjustment took a toll on her. "It was the hardest part of my life."

## School Experiences

Due to the stress, Casandra admitted to struggling with an eating disorder. "When I came to the United States, I stopped eating food. I even experienced anorexia. It was really hard. . . . I just stopped eating." She reflected on how difficult it was to be a teenager, especially in a new country with a new language. Even worse, she wasn't even sure if anyone noticed. This went on for about a year and she lost a lot of weight, which resulted in additional health issues, such as losing some of her hair. Looking back, she said, "I wish I had that support. I wish they knew that I needed help in my personal life . . . and I wish they had asked, 'Are you okay?'"

Casandra described herself as shy and expressed how difficult it was to make friends at first. She felt that focusing on her schoolwork, combined with her shyness and anorexia, led her to avoid social interactions. She would talk to her classmates but did not consider them friends. This went on for almost two years after her arrival in the United States. "My second semester sophomore year I started joining cross country and track and field and that's where I met some friends. . . . They speak English as their first language and some of them speak Spanish but . . . I met friends and that's where I got support as well. They helped me a lot." She shared that having a supportive coach also made a difference.

> Casandra encourages those who work with newcomers to get to know them, build relationships with them, and make them feel as though they belong, which is what made all the difference for her. "I felt welcome," she said. "I thought I was part of that group and I felt like, 'I belong in this room.'"

Joining a team and making friends were bright spots in Casandra's experiences. In addition, she lit up when she started talking about her English teacher, who she described as "the best." "She provided all the support to her newcomer students and non-English-speaking students. If I didn't understand, I would ask her and she would provide her time and even stay after school with me. If I ever needed anything, any extra support . . . not only with her classes but with other classes like math, even though she's not a math teacher, she would try and explain."

## Advice to Teachers

It is clear through Casandra's story that both academic and social-emotional support were essential for her transition to life in the United States. With respect to academics, and learning English specifically, repetition and help with pronunciation were most valuable to Casandra. Her teacher "had these books where you can pronounce the word and the sound. She would say, 'Repeat after me,' and that was really helpful because I struggled with pronunciation. 'Repeat after me,' and she did that every single day."

With respect to social and emotional needs, Casandra encourages those who work with newcomers to get to know them, build relationships with them, and make them feel as though they belong, which is what made all the difference for her. "I felt welcome," she said. "I thought I was part of that group and I felt like, 'I belong in this room.' I built that relationship with [that teacher] and she was a great teacher." This teacher went above and beyond, too, to help her sign up for cross country, where she was able to make friends and focus more on getting healthy.

Finally, Casandra wished that more of her teachers had shown interest and care by asking more questions. "It goes beyond support in school with homework. Mental health support is also extremely important." She wanted them to try and get to know her and other newcomers and ask simple things like, "How are you doing?" or "How can I help you?" or "Is there anything you need?" and "build that relationship" with them.

## Advice to Other Newcomers

Casandra has similar advice for other newcomers. "I would say to seek support. Ask for help. Ask the questions. I think that is the key. It doesn't matter if you're right or wrong, just ask. Ask for support if you need help with anything. Get that connection with your teachers, not just the teachers you get along with, but all your teachers. And stay after school. Oftentimes they have extra support or tutoring after school. . . . Build that relationship with your teachers—not just with school, but if you are experiencing a health problem or a family problem, seek help. . . . And get involved with sports or different activities—something that you enjoy doing. It helps you relieve stress and meet new friends."

# CAMILA AND SOFÍA

"I remember my mom brought me in and I kind of didn't want to leave her. But I was also excited about the first day because when I was in Guatemala, I also loved my first day."

| | |
|---|---|
| Ages Upon Arrival:<br>**Camila, 6; Sofía, 5** | Countries of Origin:<br>**Guatemala and Mexico** |
| Grade Upon Arrival:<br>**Camila, 1st Grade; Sofía, Kindergarten** | Home Language:<br>**Spanish** |

## Background

Camila was born in Guatemala, and Sofía was born in Tijuana, Mexico. They were both newcomers at the same elementary school in California, in first grade and kindergarten respectively. Reflecting on her home country, Camila shared, "I remember that I had friends and obviously they all spoke Spanish. When we went to school, I had my two best friends that lived next to me. I was in kindergarten and one was in first [grade] and the other one was also in kindergarten." She remembered riding her bike more in Guatemala and how sometimes she would ride her bike home from school. Sofía also shared memories about school in Mexico. "I remember my school and my teacher. The school only had one floor. And it had games and a sandbox." She described her teacher as her "favorite" because she was "really kind." Like Camila, Sofía also reminisced about her friends.

## The Journey

Camila came to the United States after she finished kindergarten in Guatemala and started first grade when she arrived. Her family took a plane to Mexico, and then her grandma picked them up. From there, they took a bus to the United States. She didn't remember much else of the journey because she fell asleep, and when she woke up, she didn't know where she was. Even though it was new and different, she felt "excited" with a desire to explore. The reason her family moved here was "because they wanted to see what it was like here and to have a better life."

Sofía vaguely remembers taking a train to get here. "I remember that we were walking near a train track," she said. She recalled feeling hungry, but not much else about the journey from Mexico to the United States. When she first arrived, she said, "I remember I felt pretty weird. And I remember my step-dad coming to get the luggage. And I remember being kind of scared next to my mom. It was only the second time I met my step-dad. My mom decided to come to the United States because my step-dad lived here."

## First Time in the United States

Camila reminisced about her first day of first grade in the United States. "I remember my mom brought me in and I . . . didn't want to leave her. But I was also excited about the first day because when I was in Guatemala I also loved my first day. I remember my teacher first showed me around the classroom and then she asked me to go to the office again and then she [returned, and then] school started." Sofía remembers being one of the students who walked Camila to the office that day. That triggered Camila's memory, who smiled, and expressed that it was helpful to have Sofía there. "She showed me where my seat was [going to] be. It felt nice because I knew where I was [going to] be and what I had to do." Having Sofía there made Camila feel more confident, too.

Sofía recalled her first day of kindergarten here in the United States. "I remember my teacher brought me to a classroom and I was really shy. And the teacher asked me to introduce myself so I just said my name. . . . Then she said, 'She talks Spanish, okay?' And then I sat down. . . . We were asked to do stuff and a lot of things I didn't understand. But then, the teacher said it in Spanish for me." Having someone who could communicate in her language put her more at ease.

## School Experiences

Both Camila and Sofía described the language barrier as the hardest part of being in a new school in a new country. "When I was in kindergarten, they changed me to another class. I think it was really a challenge because [the teacher] talked to me in English and I didn't understand." They had to communicate through gestures. "She would point to stuff and I [sort] of understood. For example, I remember she said to sit on a chair and she said it in English, and I didn't understand. Then she pointed to sit on it, and I kind of understood."

For Camila, her designated ELD time (discussed in greater detail in Designated English Language Development, pages 117–137) was initially a struggle because it was all in English. "The hardest part for me was . . . my teacher had a small group of people that didn't speak English very well and she was teaching them. She had them at a little table. The rest of the class was doing assignments while we were in the little group. And she was teaching us how to speak English and it was more challenging with the homework because I didn't really understand it. I wasn't good at subtracting because I didn't know how to [do it]. So it was harder because she left me some homework that was in English, and I had to do little parts in English."

> Sofía remembers other students in her class would try to speak Spanish to her, even if they didn't really know the language. It made her feel good to know that they were trying to connect with her, and it also helped her to understand them a bit better.

In addition to learning English, making friends at their new school was important to both Camila and Sofía. Camila's teacher encouraged her to make new friends by playing with them on the playground and drawing with them in the classroom. Basically, if anyone asked her to join them in an activity, her teacher advised her to say, "Yes." Camila took that advice and ended up making some friends, which helped her adjust. Sofía remembers other students in her class would try to speak Spanish to her, even if they didn't really know the language. It made her feel good to know that they were trying to connect with her, and it also helped her to understand them a bit better. When a new student arrived in school who also spoke Spanish, Sofía was excited to become friends with them, too.

Camila's and Sofía's initial challenges turned into successes with the support and encouragement of their teachers. They were able to learn English and make friends over time, which made both of them very proud. Camila even said that her redesignation (being considered fluent in English) in third grade was one of her greatest successes. "I remember in second grade my teacher saying we were [going to] take a test. Not all the students, just specific students [who] didn't really know English but [who sort of] knew it. And then in third grade I kind of graduated so I could be in only English classes."

##  Advice to Teachers

When it came to learning English, Camila and Sofía appreciated the support they received in their first language. Camila's teacher "would help us build word sounds . . . and we were spelling and sounding it out. And she would give pictures with examples and ask things like, 'What is he doing?' And then we would say it in Spanish and she [would say], 'Okay, and in English it's called this.'" She really liked being able to say things in Spanish first and then learn how to say them in English. "[The teacher] also kind of helped me because she gave me a card that had *she, he, we, you,* and *I* [written on them]. She gave me examples of what [each one] was. And on the back [it was written in] Spanish so I knew what it was." Camila mentioned how helpful those cards were and that she still has them.

In addition to the important first language support, Camila and Sofía also shared that their teachers held high expectations and encouraged them to speak in English so they would learn faster, which they felt they did. Having lots of opportunities to talk to people in English in school and outside of school, such as ordering food, helped Sofía learn English.

Finally, both girls emphasized the importance of time. They wished their teachers knew that it wasn't easy and that newcomer students need more time. There is a lot of information and there are a lot of new words coming at them all at once. They need more time to process what is being said and more time to practice. They also needed to hear words, and everything, repeated over and over. "Sometimes it feels like by the time we figured something out, the teacher would be moving on to something else." Time is the greatest gift a teacher can give.

## Advice to Other Newcomers

Camila's and Sofía's advice to other newcomer students was short and sweet: "Ask questions, talk as much as you can in English, practice, and do your best to learn new words." And even though they did not say this specifically, they clearly appreciated Camila's teacher's advice: When another student asks you to join them, say, "Yes."

# The Gonzalez Family: Julieta, Sebastian, Emilia, Gabriel, and Diego

"I really liked the group of friends that supported me and helped me. If everyone could be like that, and not everyone is like that, that would be a lot better."

| Ages Upon Arrival: | Country of Origin: |
|---|---|
| Julieta, 12; Sebastian, 12; Emilia, 9; Gabriel, 9; Diego, 3 | United States |

| Grades Upon Arrival: | Home Language: |
|---|---|
| Julieta, 7th grade; Sebastian, 7th grade; Emilia, 5th grade; Gabriel, 4th grade; Diego, preschool | English |

The following collection of stories is like the others, but with a twist. These five students, ranging in grade level upon arrival from preschool to seventh grade, were newcomers in Mexico, not in the United States. Their stories, while situated in a different country and involving a different target language, were surprisingly similar. This speaks to the fact that while there is diversity in all newcomers' lived experiences, there are common themes from which we can draw. We can learn from the commonalities to gain deeper insights into the newcomer experience as a whole.

## Background

The Gonzalez parents met at the University of Illinois, where Mrs. Gonzalez was studying, and Mr. Gonzalez was an exchange student from Mexico. They were both part of the university's international club, and since Mrs. Gonzalez had just come

back from studying abroad in Spain, they were matched up as "buddies." They fell in love and got married. Shortly thereafter, they moved to London and lived there for a couple of years while Mr. Gonzalez was waiting for his green card. They then moved back to the United States and lived in the Chicago area, where they had their first daughter, Julieta. About two and a half years later, they had their second daughter, Emilia. That same year, they adopted Sebastian (who was three-and-a-half years old at the time) from China. Mr. Gonzalez's job transferred the family to Houston, Texas, where they adopted Gabriel from Ethiopia as a three-year-old. They stayed in Houston for eight years, during which they became foster parents to Diego for a year and a half and then adopted him when he was two years old. About a year later, they decided to move to Merida, Mexico. They had spent several summers in Mexico and one in Peru, but felt as though this would be a great opportunity to fully immerse the kids in Spanish to strengthen their reading, writing, and speaking skills.

## First Time in Mexico

Each of the five children in the family shared what it was like being a newcomer from the United States in Mexico: It was an overwhelming feeling to start. Julieta claimed to be "the most expressive about not moving" to Mexico because she "did not want to go." When she first arrived, she described being "in shock" and wondered what was going on. "The school system is very different there, especially things like the language," she said. "It was just so hard. I was only focusing on learning the language and what's going on in school so that's why I'm a little behind now, but I'm catching up." In Gabriel's words, "It was very hard because you're just in a new country, and then it's hard when you move somewhere and you're used to everyone speaking English and then all of a sudden, everyone speaks Spanish . . . you'd say something in English and they look at you weird." Emilia felt "confused: It was just really different—the weather, the lifestyle, the houses—all the houses were different colors, and I didn't know what was going on. Everything was just really different." Whereas most of the older Gonzalez kids discussed the difficulties, Diego, the youngest, described his initial memories as "happy." He enjoyed playing with his new friends and eating rice with milk. Julieta and Emilia described one particular memory of those initial experiences: "It was the night before the first day of school and the power went out. It was summer and really hot with no air conditioning, and we had to sleep three in a single bed—two of us and our mom in one queen bed, and two boys in the other room in a single [bed]. Our little brother Diego would sleep on a couch [and] his legs would hang off. So that was the worst."

When they moved to their house, things didn't necessarily improve: "The windows were plastic—you could poke through—and the mosquitos! Our neighbors had a couple of roosters that would scream at . . . midnight or . . . two o'clock in the morning. And they had turkeys and dogs that would fight. We could hear perfectly through the plastic. And then we had to sleep on the ground. Our parents took the bed and the mattresses still had their plastic on it so we were, like, sleeping on plastic."

Mrs. Gonzalez, who works with newcomers in the United States, said the family's experiences were similar to those of her current newcomer students' experiences. Things got much easier and better with time, once they learned more of the language, made friends, and got used to their new environment.

## School Experiences

Adjusting to a new country, language, and culture brought many challenges and many successes. "The hardest part of the experience was adapting to the new environment because you're in a whole new place, you have to live in a whole new house, and speak with a whole new people. That was probably the hardest. But it also was what helped me the most, too," Gabriel shared. Sebastian agreed that one of the hardest parts for him was "adapting" because "speaking the language fluently" was a struggle. Like Gabriel, Sebastian indicated that the hardest parts were in some ways the most helpful, too. "[Learning the language] was probably the hardest and the best thing" because you can use the new language to listen to music, make friends, and communicate with others.

Emilia and Julieta shared a vivid memory about a time when the language barrier presented a big issue. Emilia set the scene: "We had to wake up at five o'clock a.m. and then we had to run to the bus stop. One day we were running across the street with our heavy backpacks and clean uniforms." Julieta explained what happened on the bus: "The bus closed on my hand. I was too embarrassed to go to the nurse, so I just walked around with a weirdly broken hand." Emilia said, "She was yelling on the bus but no one knew what was happening." Julieta reiterated that she was "too embarrassed to go to the nurse because she didn't know the language." They laugh about it now, but at the time, it was a frightening experience.

Their youngest brother, Diego, struggled in the beginning, too, due to the language barrier. There were kids in his preschool who used to bother him by pulling the curls in his hair. His mom shared, "He used to get really mad since he couldn't speak Spanish yet and would throw chairs and tables and had a really hard transition time." After they taught him a few phrases in Spanish that translated to, "Please don't touch me," or "Don't touch my hair," things got a little easier because he could express himself more. Diego agreed that it was frustrating. "I didn't like it," he said.

Over time, struggles turned to successes. Gabriel said having people to talk to made a "big impact" on him. There was one teacher who spoke both English and Spanish. "That really did help me because it was that one person that spoke English to me." Feeling as though you can understand and be understood is important.

Sebastian mentioned that "listening to music and having that musical tone" helped him a lot. Not only did it help with learning the language, but with friendships, too. Gabriel echoed Sebastian's thoughts. "A lot of music that's popular in Mexico has both English and Spanish words . . . and you [realize], 'Oh, so this means that and that means this.'" Music has built in repetition, too, which fosters greater language development.

Learning a second language, while challenging, is also something to celebrate. Diego was proud to share that what he liked most about school was being bilingual: "I loved that I could learn from my teacher. She would read us books," he said. She read in both Spanish and English, which made him happy. His favorite story was *The Boy Who Cried Wolf.* Diego was also excited to report that he was the tallest in his class.

> Sebastian and Gabriel both enjoyed playing sports and getting involved in clubs, which included soccer, basketball, baseball, chess, and Boy Scouts. Being involved helped the children feel more connected, provided opportunities to use and learn Spanish, and helped them make friends.

Outside of academics, all of the kids were involved in activities, which fostered greater connections and overall success. Sebastian and Gabriel both enjoyed playing sports and getting involved in clubs, which included soccer, basketball, baseball, chess, and Boy Scouts. Being involved helped the children feel more connected, provided opportunities to use and learn Spanish, and helped them make friends.

Emilia felt as though dance helped her learn the language and increase her confidence. The dance club was for elementary students and Emilia, in fifth grade, was one of the oldest in the club. "They were all so little so they were at my speaking level. I felt so much better there." Emilia helped the dance teacher with the younger students, which was a positive experience, too. While Julieta didn't dance, she was involved in track and field and cheer, which helped push her out of her comfort zone, meet new people, and use the language more.

Julieta and Emilia recalled the community had "cool events every Sunday" when they closed off the streets and people biked around town. There were food stands and everyone brought their dogs and enjoyed being together. They also enjoyed the *cenotes*, which are like pools in caves, and beaches.

## Advice to Teachers

Getting involved, making friends, and learning the language were themes that emerged throughout the Gonzalez family's stories. Of course, the support from teachers made a positive impact, too. Gabriel said it helped him when his teachers wrote words on the board in addition to saying them out loud. He was also allowed to take materials home to have more time and get help as needed. In addition, Gabriel discussed the importance of feeling supported, especially because he felt some of the kids at school just did not understand. "They didn't really understand how I didn't know Spanish . . . I really liked the group of friends that supported me and helped me. If everyone could be like that, and not everyone is like that, that would be a lot better." That need for belonging cannot be underestimated.

Sebastian said, "The teachers really tried to help me. Especially one teacher who was sort of funny. That helped me." After all, who doesn't want to have a little fun in class?

Like Sebastian, Emilia mentioned a specific teacher who stood out. "In fifth grade, I had this really amazing teacher. She was so nice. She always helped me. Whenever I really didn't understand anything and it was really important, she would pull out her phone and get Google Translate so I could really understand. And before I went home, she would make sure I understood the homework."

Julieta's seventh-grade biology teacher stood out the most. "Literally every single test she would sit right next to me and explain it in every possible way she could until I got it. And actually, I got the highest grade in the class, which was really fun." Julieta also recalled that one of her classmates shared her notes, which Julieta would take home and translate. "The teachers let me sit next to her," she explained, which gave her a better chance of understanding. Having a buddy and a supportive teacher was helpful.

While the Gonzalez family shared several strategies that helped them, there were a couple of things that might have helped them more. Julieta wished she had been assigned a partner, or buddy, to help her when she arrived. "I just had to figure it out," she said. The buddy system was something that happened at the elementary level, but not the secondary level. Finally, Diego remembered that there was a kid in his class who called him names. It would have helped him more if his teacher knew about it and had advocated for him.

Reflecting on their experiences, the Gonzalez family shared some highlights. Remember how Julieta was vocal about not wanting to move to Mexico? Well, in the end, she "was the one who wanted to stay." Sebastian and Gabriel admitted that they, too, did not initially want to move, but looking back now, they are grateful for the experience. Gabriel said, "I'm really happy I did have that experience…I look back on it and say, 'Man, I'm glad I did that because it's really helping me.' Even if I hated it at the time." Learning more Spanish and being able to communicate more with his dad's relatives were highlights. Emilia described the experience of being a newcomer as "successful" because in addition to learning a new language and experiencing a new culture, she gained confidence, too. As for Diego, he plans to move back to Mexico to be reunited with his friends and toys.

## Advice to Other Newcomers

From those reflections, the Gonzalez family shared words of encouragement for other newcomers. Even if you may be resistant to the idea of moving to a new country and speaking a new language, hang in there and give it time. As for specific suggestions, the Gonzalez children recommend getting involved in activities, listening to bilingual music, reading bilingual books, making friends, and trying hard to learn the language. "It will be hard at times, but also great." Through this experience, they learned that they can get through anything. Their advice to other newcomers: Do not give up and know that you can get through it, too. You've got this!

# Summary

Through all of the unique narratives, it is abundantly clear that what made the most positive impact on these newcomers' experiences was human connection and relationships. Once relationships were established, true learning was able to happen. As Maya Angelou so eloquently stated, "People will forget what you said. People will forget what you did. But people will never forget how you made them feel." Making newcomers feel safe and welcome is paramount. We start that process by getting to know them. We were honored to have had the opportunity to get to know this group of newcomers on a deeper level as they shared their stories. They taught us so much about the diversity of newcomers' experiences while also allowing us to discover common challenges and successes. To conclude, we want to highlight several strategies that positively impacted their experiences and their learning. These are listed below in figure 2.1.

Figure 2.1—Recommendations from Newcomers

**What Newcomers Need**

- Teachers who care
- Teachers as advocates
- Patient teachers
- Encouraging teachers
- Teachers who hold high expectations
- Support personnel like paraprofessionals (bilingual if available)
- Counselors (bilingual if available)
- Supportive coaches
- Educators who value all forms of cultural and linguistic diversity

**Effective Classroom Practices**

- Know students' names and pronounce them correctly.
- Get to know your learners and find ways to connect with them.
- Include content that is interesting and engaging.
- Give fewer lectures that don't account for language needs.
- Allow extra time (wait time, processing time).

*(Continued)*

Figure 2.1—Recommendations from Newcomers (Continued)

- Provide primary language support as appropriate.
- Have multilingual and/or translation tools available (bilingual dictionary, translator).
- Get students involved in extracurricular activities.
- Emphasize vocabulary instruction and repeat key vocabulary throughout.
- Repeat instructions.
- Write instructions on the board in addition to saying them orally.
- Provide opportunities for newcomers to feel successful in something they are good at.
- Practice purposeful partnering.
- Assign buddies.
- Include opportunities to talk with different people in English.
- Help them feel like they belong.
- Use gestures.
- Provide visual support.

**Advice for Other Newcomers**

- Watch television in English.
- Get involved in sports, clubs, or other extracurricular activities.
- Reach out to your teachers.
- Ask for help.
- Be a friend to other ELs and newcomers.
- Find opportunities to practice using English outside of school.
- Listen to music in English (or bilingual music).
- Take materials home to practice when you have more time.
- Keep trying, and don't give up!

## Reflection Questions

- How do you learn about the backgrounds and stories of your newcomer students?

- What opportunities do newcomers have to connect with other students and other teachers?

- What are some ways your classroom environment supports newcomers?

- What support structures are in place for your newcomers and how are they communicated?

# CHAPTER 3

# Social and Emotional Considerations for Newcomers

Many newcomers fled traumatic situations in their home countries. Some came to the United States with family members and others came alone. Regardless of the circumstances, they all have one thing in common—being new. They are new to the country, the language, and the culture. The school system is also different, which can make it difficult to navigate at first. This combination of factors has the potential to induce stress and anxiety, which can take an emotional toll on newcomers. We turn again to the power of story to help us better understand how newcomers might feel during those first days and months. These stories emphasize the importance of supporting not only newcomers' academic and language development, but their social-emotional well-being too. We offer strategies and tips throughout this chapter for creating safe environments where students feel connected and have a sense of belonging, which lead to more positive outcomes—social, emotional, and academic.

## The Need to Feel Safe

While a few newcomers expressed a sense of excitement upon arrival in the U.S., the majority expressed varying levels of fear, anxiety, uncertainty, and insecurity. When Camila, who had just finished kindergarten in Guatemala, first arrived, she remembers being scared. She did not remember much of the journey to get to the United States, but she did remember falling asleep and then waking up and not knowing where she was, which was terrifying. Imagine being so young and scared and then showing up for your first day of school not knowing anyone, or the language, or the culture, or the school system. It is easy for that fear to take over. This is where teachers come in as the first faces that many of our students see. We have the power to make a difference by helping them feel safe, welcome, and cared for. It is the informal caring relationships we establish with newcomers that matter most (U.S. Department of Education 2016).

## THREATS TO SAFETY IN THE CLASSROOM

"It was our first lockdown drill of the school year. The voice came over the loudspeaker that my students did not understand. The doors were locked and the lights turned off as we huddled in the corner of the classroom. I will never forget the look of terror on my students' faces. Even though I explained that it was 'just a drill,' the emotional trauma of their past had been triggered. Some of them had recently fled a situation in which they were afraid of getting shot on their way to school."

—High School ELD Teacher

"The librarian was decorating the library and she popped a balloon right next to one of our refugees from Eritrea, who had been incarcerated for years and tortured. He was completely triggered by the loud noise—it's just the little things that you need to be aware of."

—High School ELD Teacher

In the scenarios described above, the stress and anxiety of the lockdown drill and the balloon popping incident essentially shut down the brain's ability to effectively process information, which can last for quite some time after the event. More importantly, the experience threatened the students' feelings of safety. Maslow's Hierarchy of Needs (1943; see figure 3.1) recognizes that first and foremost, our physiological needs (e.g., air, food, water) must be met. Safety comes next. Hammond reminds us that "we cannot downplay students' need to feel safe and valued in the classroom" (2015, 47). Our brains are wired in a way that seeks to keep us safe, and alive, at all costs. This is often referred to as the "fight or flight" phenomenon, which is where the mind and body intersect. When we do not feel safe, our bodies produce stress hormones that make it nearly impossible to learn (Hammond 2015). This is similar to Krashen's Affective Filter Hypothesis, which states that if we feel anxious or stressed, a "filter" or barrier pops up, blocking learning and language development (1982). Being aware of this process is the first step. The next step is to create an environment in which our students feel safe.

Figure 3.1—Maslow's Hierarchy of Needs

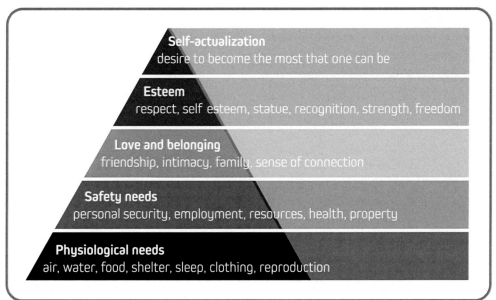

**Self-actualization**
desire to become the most that one can be

**Esteem**
respect, self esteem, statue, recognition, strength, freedom

**Love and belonging**
friendship, intimacy, family, sense of connection

**Safety needs**
personal security, employment, resources, health, property

**Physiological needs**
air, water, food, shelter, sleep, clothing, reproduction

## Preparing for Emergency Drills

Lockdown drills are common in twenty-first-century classrooms. They can instill feelings of insecurity for all students, but particularly those who have experienced trauma. While you cannot prevent the traumatic feelings, you can prepare for them. Go to the front office and request a list of drills in advance so you can be prepared to support the students for whom an event like that can trigger emotional trauma. For example, plan a calm activity just before or just after a scheduled drill, so students' anxiety levels will be lowered.

We may not know in advance when a student may be triggered emotionally. For example, you may be doing a unit or activity that includes content that could be triggering, such as racism, death, abuse, or war. Those triggers will vary from student to student based on their experiences. The more we learn from our students about their potential triggers, the better prepared we can be when those moments arise.

{ "They have so much trauma. [One] girl was in my auto class and I didn't know this, but her brother died from carbon monoxide poisoning in an accident in a mechanic shop. So we're in this mechanic shop and she was having panic attacks, and she wouldn't engage, and she wouldn't do anything. And then finally, once I got to know her, [I asked,] 'Why are you in this class? You shouldn't be in this class.' If I [had not] gotten to know her, then I would have never known [about her trauma] the whole semester. I would have just [felt,] 'She never wants to do anything.'"

—High School ELD Teacher }

72

"We had child soldiers from Myanmar (Burma) and Rangoon at one point. They were being persecuted in their country, and they were trained to defend themselves and their families. With them, my biggest concern was figuring what their triggers were and making other students aware of what those triggers were because, I mean, those were kids that were trained to kill with their hands. So we did not want them triggered at school. They came through a different agency at the time but they were well supported. It took about six, seven months until they began to function. But that was challenging in different ways, because first [they] have triggers, and then they didn't have an understanding that girls have the right to be at school. So they were hugely freaked out by the fact that girls were in school. [You] start with, 'This is the girls' bathroom, you don't go in there, alright?' They had to learn all the rules from scratch."

—High School ELD Teacher

## Alternate Assignments and Safe Places

Have alternate assignments or activities ready to go in case of content triggers. For example, if you are doing a unit on war and the battle-related portions trigger one of your students, prepare an alternate activity, such as researching the efforts on the home front or a geography lesson on the countries involved. It is also a good idea to have a safe place for a student to go in case of emotional triggers, such as a different classroom, the counselor's office, the library, or maybe just outside the classroom in the hallway. For younger students, having a calm corner within the classroom with a box of stuffed animals or sensory and fidget tools might provide comfort as well.

## THREATS TO SAFETY BEYOND THE CLASSROOM

Creating a safe classroom environment and being prepared for triggering content or events are essential to providing the support that newcomers, and all students for that matter, need. However, it is important to note that many of these emotions are being triggered outside of school, which we cannot readily see. What we might see is a student who seems distracted, withdrawn, sad, or angry.

> "Carlos always seemed a bit distracted in class. As we got to know one another and he started to trust me, he shared more of his story with me. His way of getting to the United States from El Salvador was by riding on the tops of trains—by himself. I had seen documentaries about how dangerous that trek is, but I had never up to that point had a student in my class who had experienced it. He almost died! I can't imagine! Then, when he arrived, he moved in with his biological parents, who he hadn't seen since he was very young. They were strangers to him. And in the time since they had left, they had had several more children and a whole new life—without him. The family dynamics were awkward and he didn't feel as though he belonged. If I had experienced that, I would be distracted in class, too."
>
> —High School ELD teacher

"Alejandra arrived at age 16 as an unaccompanied minor. Her journey to the United States from El Salvador was long and dangerous. She was detained in Mexico and had to spend several months in a group home there. When she finally arrived, she moved in with her biological father, whom she didn't know because he left El Salvador when Alejandra was just an infant. And even though he was her biological father, she expressed fear that he was going to rape her. In her mind, she was living with a strange man! She eventually moved out. From that point forward, she was on her own. She would come to school during the day and work at night. Her weekends were spent working, cleaning, doing laundry, and grocery shopping. Whenever I think of strength and resilience, I think of Alejandra."

—High school ELD teacher

It takes time and consistent effort to form positive teacher-student connections, which are built upon the foundation of trust. Since Carlos did not have a solid support system in place outside of school, it was even more important to provide that network of support within the school. Had the teacher not learned about Carlos's story, she may have made other assumptions about why Carlos was distracted in class. This serves as another good reminder to get to know our learners and their stories. Experiences outside of class can impact what is happening in the classroom. Alejandra's safety and security felt threatened, even though she was living with a family member. To be young and on your own would make coming to school and focusing extremely challenging. With the proper support, though, students like Alejandra can persevere.

## BUILDING TRUST AND CHECKING IN ON EMOTIONAL WELL-BEING

Building trust does not happen overnight. Newcomers probably will not tell you everything about themselves on the first day. And if you do not speak their home language, it may take even more time to establish that relationship and learn more about them, but it is worth the time and effort.

> "You need to build a relationship with the kids before you can teach them anything. I had a huge debate with a teacher who took over my job at a previous school and she called me and she said, 'I don't know what to do. These kids won't work for me.' And I told her, 'I know they can [do it] because they have done it before. What have you done to build a relationship with them?' And her words were, 'I don't have to build a relationship with them. I just have to teach them.' At which point I said, 'Well, good luck.' Then I started getting text messages from those [students] saying, 'We'll have her gone by Christmas.' And I said, 'No, you won't.' [Newcomers are] a very specific population that relies on relationships, more than other populations, due to a general mistrust, trauma, confusion—all of those emotional things that they go through. If you're not a safe person, they will not work with you."
>
> —High School ELD teacher

How do you build a relationship with a student when you do not share a common language? There are many things that can be done from day one. In fact, more than 70 percent of our communication is nonverbal (Burgoon, Manusov, and Guerrero 2021). Our body language, our tone of voice, and our use of gestures serve as great starting points.

Here are a few strategies for building trust and checking in on students' well-being. (URLs for videos showing these strategies in action can be found in Resources on page 239.)

## Greeting Students at the Door

You are the first face students see when they enter the classroom. By greeting them at the door, you send the message that you see them and that you care about them. Even a smile and calm, welcoming tone of voice can go a long way. You can simply make eye contact, smile, and say "good morning" or "good afternoon" or "welcome." Or you can offer a handshake, fist bump, or high five. If you are brave, you might even create a special handshake for each student. Whatever method you choose, you are sending the message to your students: "I'm glad you are here."

## Cultural Considerations

Be mindful that, in some cultures, direct eye contact can be viewed as disrespectful. In other cultures, it is not okay to have physical contact, particularly with those of the opposite gender. Therefore, always have options based on how students are most comfortable greeting you.

## Morning Meetings/Dialogue Circles

Checking in as a group during a morning meeting or start-of-class dialogue circle is time well spent. Provide an opportunity to share feelings and connect. Include get-to-know-you activities, which seek to build community within the classroom. For example, have students pick a number between 1 and 5, where 1 represents feeling bad and 5 represents feeling really good, with everything else in between. Give them the choice to share why they chose the number they did if they are comfortable.

## The Mood Meter

Based on the RULER approach to social-emotional learning (Yale Center for Emotional Intelligence 2022), the Mood Meter is a color-coded grid. From top to bottom represents the level of energy, and from left to right represents the level of pleasantness. Therefore, the top right quadrant (yellow) is high energy with very pleasant emotions (e.g., excited). The top left quadrant (red) is high energy with unpleasant emotions (e.g., angry). The lower left quadrant (blue) represents low energy and unpleasant emotions (e.g., sad, tired). And finally, the lower right quadrant (green) involves lower energy with pleasant emotions (e.g., calm, content, ready to learn).

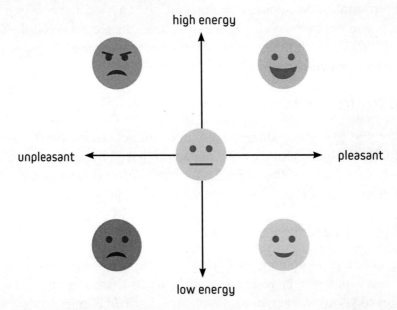

For students who do not (*yet*) have the words in English to express themselves, use emojis such as the ones in the Mood Meter or provide an opportunity for students to point to an image. The emojis pictured are universal, so students should be able to identify one that best represents how they are feeling.

**emojis**—*pictographs of faces, objects, or symbols*

Provide some first language (L1) support for emotion words so students understand what these emojis represent on a deeper level. As an added benefit, students develop additional vocabulary words related to their emotions and/or how they are feeling.

**Emotion Words Mood Meter**

| | | | | | |
|---|---|---|---|---|---|
| angry | tense | annoyed | happy | excited | upbeat |
| frustrated | nervous | worried | energized | motivated | cheerful |
| troubled | furious | shocked | lively | joyful | thrilled |
| sad | disappointed | mopey | calm | mellow | loving |
| lonely | tired | ashamed | peaceful | grateful | carefree |
| alone | bored | uneasy | content | relaxed | comfy |

energy level

pleasantness level

In many cases, what students really need and want is simply for someone to ask them how they are doing and check in on them. Sending the message that they are seen, valued, and cared about fosters feelings of connection, trust, and belonging.

> **Casandra:** "I wish (my teachers) knew that I needed help in my personal life . . . and I wish they had asked, 'Are you okay?'"

There are several resources for grade-level appropriate social-emotional learning tips and strategies for how you can implement activities such as this in the classroom. See Resources, page 239, for additional ideas.

## The Need for Belonging

> **Mariama:** "They looked at me like I was a terrorist." As the only Muslim girl at her school, Mariama felt "different from everyone else." When it was Mariama's turn to have her picture taken for her school identification card, the photographer asked her to uncover her head. It was a school rule, after all. Mariama had not developed enough English yet to fully understand the request. It was clear that the photographer did not understand the cultural significance and importance of a Muslim female keeping her head covered in public.

This was just one of the many times Mariama felt like an outsider, and shows how being "different" caused her at times to feel as though she did not belong. Mariama eventually stopped wearing her hijab. Not only is it difficult to adjust to a new culture and a new language, but to feel the need to compromise your identity to "fit in" can take an additional toll on students' mental health and social-emotional well-being.

> "I had a newcomer in third grade, and [his] parent said that he would go home crying because in the yard it was hard for him to communicate with the students, even though a lot of them spoke Spanish. He just felt that he didn't have the language to fully incorporate himself into the group with the students. His mom would say he would come home and just cry thinking he had no friends, even though a lot of the kids do speak Spanish at our school. But I think it was a frustration of feeling like he didn't know what was going on around him."
>
> —Elementary School Teacher

Returning to Maslow's hierarchy of needs, after physiological and safety needs comes the need for love and belonging (1943). We all want to feel loved, like we belong, and that we are accepted. Each student who shared their story expressed this in some way.

> **Eva and Aaron:** "I just remember really wanting to talk to people, but I didn't really know English, so it was really hard. I just couldn't be myself because I couldn't express what I felt," Eva lamented. Aaron struggled with this, too. "I always just wanted to be a normal student. . . . I didn't like that I was outside of everything. I just wanted to be like everybody else."

Many newcomers expressed similar sentiments. They shared that initially, they did not feel like themselves in this new language and culture because they could not fully show the world who they were. When students of all ages feel as though they are "on the outside" or "different" or "alone," particularly due to linguistic or cultural differences, their sense of belonging is compromised. Being seen leads to a greater sense of belonging.

**Cristina:** Cristina felt as though her teachers never saw her attributes or capacity. "I don't think they saw me. Because I couldn't show them who I was." She was interested in acting and drama in her home country of Colombia. However, her drama class in the United States was very difficult for her because of all the reading and memorization of English words that she did not know (yet). For one assignment she was allowed to pick any character to portray, so she chose to be a mime. She felt good about her performance and, in a way, accomplished. It was at that moment that the drama teacher's demeanor changed, as if somehow, all of a sudden, she saw Cristina as intelligent and capable because the language barrier was removed.

## MAKING FRIENDS

One of the most common struggles reported by newcomers is making friends, which is also part of belonging.

**Camila and Sofía:** Camila and Sofía reminisced about their lives in Guatemala and Mexico and remembered having friends there. They missed their friends. But there were challenges to making friends in the United States. Her teacher encouraged Camila to interact with other kids in the class and said if they asked her to play soccer, she should play. Even though she admitted to not knowing how to play, Camila said yes so she could make friends. For Sofía, some students tried to speak Spanish to her, which helped her connect with her classmates on some level.

The voices and experiences of newcomers emphasized that the two most effective ways for helping them connect with others and fostering that sense of belonging were first, by creating a classroom community where everyone felt valued and accepted, and second, by encouraging them to get involved with activities outside of school.

## CREATING A POSITIVE CLASSROOM COMMUNITY

Relationships and connections within and beyond the classroom are foundational to the academic success and social-emotional well-being of students. The research supports what newcomers shared with us—one teacher can make a difference. We can create identity-safe spaces where all students feel accepted for who they are (Hammond 2015). Below are a few examples from the wealth of insights students shared emphasizing the critical role of the positive physical and emotional space that teachers created within the classroom.

**Cristina:** "It didn't matter if we came from another country or had different levels of skill in the English language. . . . It was a friendly space for me. . . a safety space where I felt seen."

**Mariama:** "It made life so much better. . . . We had [our teachers] and small classes. And even if you make a mistake or anything, no one laughed—it was great. English class was a safe and comfortable environment, which was extremely important."

**Casandra:** "I felt welcome. . . . I thought I was part of that group, and I felt like 'I belong in this room.' I built that relationship with her, and she was a great teacher."

**Eva:** "They believed in me, even when I didn't believe in myself."

**Aaron:** "In ELL class we all went through the same thing and could relate to one another. It was a safe place where I felt more normal. And because of that, me and my classmates became better friends."

**Babacar:** "We knew that [the teachers] cared about us learning and [they] really invested time into helping us.... We were building a family there."

**Sebastian:** "The teachers really tried to help me. Especially one teacher who was sort of funny. That helped me."

**Emilia:** "In fifth grade I had this really amazing teacher. She was so nice. She always helped me. Whenever I really didn't understand anything and it was really important, she would pull out her phone and get Google Translate so I could really understand. And before I went home, she would make sure I understood the homework."

Create a positive classroom environment, and build community (or, as Babacar said, *family*). Taking time to get to know one another in the classroom is time well spent.

## Windows and Mirrors

Reflect students' languages and cultures in classroom materials and resources to send the message that linguistic and cultural diversity are valued in the classroom. Label objects with all students' languages, create word walls, have bilingual dictionaries available, use posters representing the backgrounds of those in your class, include relatable scenarios and familiar names in math word problems and other readings, bring in pieces of art and music from other countries, and play games from around the world. Choose books and other materials where students can see themselves reflected (*mirrors*) as well as learn about the experiences of others (*windows*) (Fleming 2019).

## Class Playlist

Music can connect us and can transcend language. We can feel the rhythm and the beat, even if we do not know the words. Create a place (written or digital) where students can add their favorite music. This activity is great for all ages. For younger learners who have not yet developed literacy, write the name of the song or artist for them. Older students can add it themselves. Then, rotate through that playlist during warm-ups, transitions, and end-of-class wrap-up or clean-up. *Note*: Because music is personal, some students may not be comfortable sharing this with everyone, so giving them the option to have their chosen music played or not will be important.

## Personal Artifact

Choosing an object that represents something about you is simple, yet deeply personal. It is amazing how much you can learn about a person by the object they choose and why they chose it. The object can be anything—a book, a pair of ballet shoes, a piece of jewelry given to them by a relative, a ticket, a trinket from travels, or a piece of art from another country. With linguistic support (e.g., sentence frames, bilingual dictionaries or electronic translators, or heritage language [L1] buddies), ask students to share using as many words or gestures as they can about the object and its meaning. This can be done virtually as well, using Flipgrid or other video-based programs. Use sentence frames as scaffolds:

- I chose_____ because____.
- This is _____ . It represents _____.

## Teach Us Your Name

Our names are part of our identities. Many newcomers have names that may not be familiar to us. However, it is critically important for us, and others in the class, to learn how to properly pronounce them. The My Name, My Identity Campaign was created by the Santa Clara County Office of Education in partnership with the National Association for Bilingual Education (**mynamemyidentity.org**), and it provides resources and activities for this topic. This can be made into a class community-building activity by having everyone share their name and how to pronounce it. And if possible, they can share what their name means, too. This can be done visually or orally.

Here are books that address the topic of names to use as starting points.

- *The Name Jar* by Yangsook Choi
- *My Name is Yoon* by Helen Recorvits
- *Alma and How She Got Her Name* by Juana Martinez-Neal
- *Your Name Is a Song* by Jamilah Thompkins-Bigelow
- *Hope* by Isabell Monk
- *How Nivi Got Her Names* by Laura Deal
- *My Name Is Bilal* by Asama Mobin-Uddin
- *My Name Is Sangoel* by Karen Williams and Khadra Mohammed
- *Teach Us Your Name* by Huda Essa

## Favorites and/or Questions-of-the-Day

Sharing favorites or fun facts is a great way to get to know each other in class. It is also quick and easy and can be incorporated as frequently or infrequently as you would like. Use during a morning meeting, in community circles, or as an end-of-the-day activity in classrooms of all ages. Discuss your favorite breakfast foods one day and your favorite music on another day. This can lead to developing a Class Playlist (see above). Another time, involve everyone by asking them to act out their favorite sport or activity. You should answer the questions, too, so everyone gets to know you as well. The students really enjoy hearing about their teachers' lives and interests. Encourage students to contribute questions or ideas. They might like to know if their classmates have pets or jobs or how many siblings they have, their favorite movie, or what language they speak at home. For newcomers and other emerging English learners, having L1 buddies or translation tools available will be helpful.

## Find Someone Who

This is a great icebreaker, but it can be used throughout the year. It is a fun way for classmates and teachers to get to know each other *and* get up and move in the classroom. Create a grid that has pictures or prompts based on likes/dislikes, hobbies/talents, past experiences, and so forth. Then, students go around the room trying to find someone who can say or nod *yes* to one of the pictures or prompts. If they do, that person adds their name (see example on the next page). Then, they move on to another person in the room. The ultimate goal is to get signatures for every square.

## BEYOND THE CLASSROOM: INVOLVEMENT IN EXTRACURRICULAR ACTIVITIES

In addition to creating connections within the classroom, it is equally important to help newcomers foster connections with others outside of the classroom—another common theme that emerged from those interviewed. Extracurricular activities can be a more relaxed way to interact with others, do something they enjoy, or try something new. These activities provide hands-on experiential learning opportunities that may not happen during academic instruction. Extracurricular activities can also provide meaningful opportunities to use and develop language.

Involvement outside of the academic classroom environment has a variety of benefits. First, there are social-emotional benefits, such as fostering connections and a sense of belonging. There are also linguistic benefits; these clubs and organizations provide meaningful opportunities to use and develop language. And finally, there are potential leadership opportunities, which can build confidence. Increased confidence can also support positive social-emotional well-being.

**Aaron and Eva:** Aaron started swimming right after arriving in the U.S., and the language barrier created challenges for him at practice. His coaches had to demonstrate what they wanted him to do. That was how they communicated. That modeling and demonstration helped him both in and out of the classroom. Eva was encouraged by her teachers to create and lead a recycling club at school, which turned into a leadership opportunity. She also became a Link Leader, which involved showing new students around the school and helping them get to know what the school was like. It felt good for her to pay it forward by being the "buddy" she had had when she was new.

**Mariama and Babacar:** Being involved in the pre-collegiate program at their high school is where Mariama and Babacar found an additional system of support and where they were able to form friendships outside of their academic classes. Babacar remembered one college visit trip that was a turning point for him in the United States. "That's when a lot of people started opening up because for the first time everybody was kind of in the same environment because everybody was away from home. Everybody was away from their friends . . . everyone was in unknown territory, and everybody definitely opened up. It was a great experience."

**Casandra:** Getting involved in extracurricular activities made a difference. "My second semester sophomore year, I started joining cross country and track and field and that's where I met some friends. . . . They speak English as their first language and some of them speak Spanish but . . . I met friends and that's where I got support as well. They helped me a lot."

## Extracurricular Activities

Find out what clubs and activities are available at the school and/or within the community. Or start your own (multilingual theater or book club, newcomers club, etc.). Encourage newcomers to get involved. Take it one step further by offering to accompany them to the first meeting or practice. If they say they are not interested in anything offered, encourage them to try something new. For example, students who come from warm climates to cold winters might not consider joining a cross-country ski team. However, if they are personally invited by a teacher at the school, they might give it a try. This may be completely out of their comfort zone, but many students find these experiences, which they never would have had if it were not for a teacher's encouragement, to be incredible, and in some cases life-changing. Remember, one person CAN make a difference.

## SUPPORTING NEWCOMERS ON THE FIRST DAY

Ensuring the social-emotional well-being of our students is at the heart of our role as educators. Helping students feel safe and have a sense of belonging are essential steps in that process. Having a plan in place will help you reach those goals more efficiently and effectively. However, sometimes those plans get shaken up a bit. Due to the circumstances surrounding many newcomers' journeys to get to the U.S., it is not uncommon for a newcomer to show up in the middle of the school year, or even toward the end. And in some cases, we may have little to no advance notice. So, what can you do to prepare? Here are a few ideas to get you started. Having these resources ready to go will help you be prepared any time newcomer students arrive in your classroom.

## Travel Book

Have a travel book available, such as *The Travel Book: A Journey Through Every Country in the World* or *The World: A Traveler's Guide to the Planet*, both by Lonely Planet. As soon as you find out which country a student is from, open the book to the section about that country. Everyone in the class can learn about where your new student is from even if they cannot tell you in English *yet*. And the newcomer can feel that immediate sense of welcome and connection.

## Translation Resources

Find out the newcomer's home language and locate a bilingual dictionary or use Google Translate or another translation program. The Google Translate app has both oral and written options. Keep in mind that these apps are not 100 percent accurate and should not be overly relied upon, but they can at least help with initial communication. Even better, if another student speaks the same language, they may be able to help. Later, when you have a bit more time, you can create a "cheat sheet" of key phrases, such as *hello, welcome*, and *How are you?*, in their home language.

## Newcomer Kit

Create a newcomer kit that will be ready and available at any point a newcomer might join your class. Here are a few suggestions about what should be included in the kit:

**Identification Card**. Have a card that you or you and the student fill out together to be carried with them throughout the day. Include their name, country of origin, language, grade, teacher, bus number (if applicable), and contact information such as a parent/guardian's phone number and address. The student can show the card as needed for help or support. Note that the type and amount of information on the card can be adapted to the specific student or context. See page 93 for one teacher's story of a time when a card like this would have come in handy.

| **Sample Identification Card** | | |
| --- | --- | --- |

Hello!

My name is _____. I am learning English.

I just arrived from _____ and speak _____.

I am in _____ grade at _____ (school).

My bus # is _____.

My address is: _____.

In case of emergency, call: _____.

**Map of the School.** Having a map of the school is beneficial to support students in finding different classrooms, the office, the school nurse, the gym, the auditorium, and the cafeteria. This is particularly helpful for secondary students who travel from room to room for their classes.

**Visual Schedule.** To help newcomers navigate their class schedules, especially at the secondary level, add a visual component to their daily schedules.

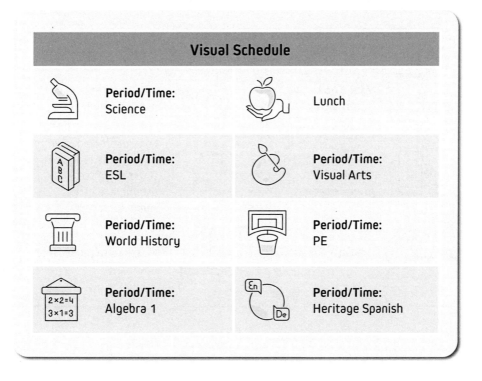

| **Visual Schedule** | |
| --- | --- |
| Period/Time: Science | Lunch |
| Period/Time: ESL | Period/Time: Visual Arts |
| Period/Time: World History | Period/Time: PE |
| Period/Time: Algebra 1 | Period/Time: Heritage Spanish |

cognates—words that have the same linguistic derivation (from the same original word or root) in two or more languages; for example, *chocolate* in English = *chocolate* in Spanish = *chocolat* in French; another example—English *is*, German *ist*, and Latin *est* are from Indo-European *esti*

**List of Cognates by Language.** Share some common age-appropriate cognates right away for a huge confidence booster. Cognates show newcomers how much they may already know in English. They will vary by grade level, content area, and language. To find cognate lists for your students' L1s, do a quick web search for "cognates between English and ____." For example, this site provides bilingual glossaries and cognates for multiple languages: **steinhardt.nyu.edu/metrocenter/language-rbern/education/bilingual-glossaries-and-cognates**. The site is arranged by subject area, grade level, and language. Here is one that provides cognates shared between English and Spanish: **spanishcognates.org**. Within this site, it is also possible to search by content area: language arts, mathematics, science, or social studies. (See Resources, page 239, for more information.)

**Basic Conversation Tool.** Provide newcomers with some starter phrases for common requests, with visual support, as a resource for expressing their needs. They can point to the visual initially as needed.

| Sample of Basic Conversation Tool | | |
|---|---|---|
| May I go to the restroom? | | Can you please speak more slowly? |
| May I use my phone? I need to call _____ (my mom, my dad). | | I am lost. I am looking for ___ (the restroom, the main office, the attendance office, room number X). |
| I have a question. | | May I go to my locker? |

"One of my students missed the bus, and he didn't know what to do because the doors were already locked at school. He thought he would just try and walk home, but it's about a 10-minute drive. Think of how long that would be! And he didn't know his address. He found the train tracks and he started walking along the train tracks and he made it to downtown. He looks a lot older than he is. He looks like a man, but he's just a kid. Someone pulled him over and [asked,] 'What are you doing?' He couldn't speak English. He spoke Quiché. So they [decided,] 'Well, we're just going to call the police.' And he was terrified that he was going to be deported. He's here without parents, and he just had no idea even where to tell him he lives. It ended up that the police came, they found someone that spoke Spanish, and [asked,] 'What are you doing?' He [said,] 'I'm trying to walk home.' 'From where?' 'From school.' 'What school do you go to?' He barely knew the word for his school. They finally figured out which school it was. So the police called [the school] and [told them,] 'We have a person—he says he's a student at [your school], he doesn't look like a high school student . . . can you talk to him?' [The person at the school asked,] '¿Quién es (who is this)?' He gives his name and explains that he's lost and doesn't know where he is. And he's speaking in broken Spanish because he speaks Quiché. [The school asked,] 'Okay, you live in the apartments, right? Okay, so we're going to tell the police to bring you to the apartments.' The police brought him, and [he] didn't even know which apartment was his. It took about 20 minutes because they all looked the same. The [police] just dropped him off at the apartments. He came here by himself as an unaccompanied minor, so I'm sure there's always that fear. I know my students are always fearful of getting in trouble or getting deported, [after] all that they went through to get here."

—High School ELD Teacher

## A FEW WORDS ABOUT ASSESSMENT

When considering a student's emotions in the learning process, we cannot forget about demonstrations of learning, or assessment. Think about how Eva described that she "freaked out" when she was asked to take her very first test. Test anxiety can be intense for students of all language proficiency levels, including dominant English speakers. Imagine how much anxiety can increase when being asked to demonstrate knowledge of something in a language in which you are not *yet* proficient. How will your newcomers who are new to English be able to show you what they know? This is a common question that many educators grapple with.

Our advice is simple: be flexible, creative, and patient. And above all, believe that your students *will* get it over time. Here are some considerations for lowering anxiety around assessment for newcomers:

- Provide L1 support as needed (e.g., a bilingual buddy, an electronic translator, a bilingual dictionary).
- Allow for choice whenever possible. Create a "choice board" with a variety of options students can choose from to show evidence of learning. Visual, kinesthetic, and auditory/oral options should be included. Below are examples. Note that some of these span multiple categories.

  Visual—poster, journal, drawing, children's book, graphic novel, scrapbook, foldable, mind map

  Kinesthetic—video, experiment, acting/role-playing, board game, matching, puppet show, three-dimensional timeline, flipbook

  Auditory/Oral—one-to-one conference, speech, song/rap, presentation, play, interview, panel discussion, commercial, news report

- Provide opportunities for students to use social language to describe an academic concept.
- Include options for collaborative projects.

There are a variety of elements to be mindful of when creating assessments. We advocate for frequent, informal comprehension checks along the way. When it comes time for more summative assessments and products, consider the choice options presented above, which will vary based on grade level and content area. Finally, we encourage you to include the voices of your students in the process. How do they feel they can successfully demonstrate learning to you? Their ideas may not only surprise you, but they may inspire you as well.

## Summary

Language, literacy, and academic development cannot happen without social-emotional well-being. To support the academic success of newcomers, we must first meet their needs for safety and belonging. Being new anywhere is stressful. Factors such as trauma, lack of safety and security, fear, anxiety, and language barriers increase that stress level tenfold. Learning about our students' experiences and potential triggers can help us create a plan of care and support. After getting to know our newcomers the best we can, have newcomer kits and materials ready for use, create a safe and welcoming classroom community, regularly check in on newcomers, help them feel connected with others in the classroom and school, encourage their involvement in extracurricular activities, be prepared with alternate assignments and activities when triggering content or events are present, and consider assessment options that set them up for success. By taking these steps, we are showing newcomers that we care, we believe in them, we support them, and we are willing to walk with them on their journey as an ally and an advocate.

## Reflection Questions

- How are newcomers welcomed at your school? In your classroom?
- How do you build a positive classroom community where all students feel safe, valued, and a sense of belonging?
- In what ways do you celebrate newcomers' accomplishments and support their challenges?
- What opportunities do you provide for newcomers to successfully demonstrate learning in a low-anxiety environment?
- If you have any concerns about your newcomers, how will you address those concerns?

# CHAPTER 4

# Strategies for Engaging Newcomer Families

> The ways schools care about children is reflected in the ways schools care about children's families.
>
> —Joyce Epstein (2019, 11)

Some newcomer students come alone as unaccompanied minors. Some end up living with relatives, while others end up living in foster care or with a sponsor. Some come with siblings, parents, grandparents, aunts, uncles, or other caregivers. It is important to consider the unique and varying circumstances of newcomers' reasons for coming to the U.S., their journeys to get here, and their living situations upon arrival. The reasons for coming typically involve either seeking better educational or economic opportunities or escaping war, violence, or political unrest (U.S. Department of Education 2016). The journey can be arduous and, in some cases, traumatic. And the living situations upon arrival are often less than ideal. Imagine being in a new country where you do not speak the language, the norms and traditions are different, and the school system is completely foreign. And then, you drop off your child at school.

While we have multiple systems of support in place for the students, we cannot forget about the needs of parents and other caregivers. In this chapter, we share tips and strategies for welcoming, supporting, engaging, and empowering newcomer families to foster positive home, school, and community partnerships. When we mention "family" or "parent," we are referring to anyone caring for the newcomer students in our classrooms.

## Welcoming Newcomer Families

When schools and teachers welcome newcomer families and collaborate with them in ways that respect and value their cultures, aspirations, and needs, while focusing on their strengths and assets, the schools and the entire community are enriched (U.S. Department of Education 2016). First and foremost, learn as much as you can about the family, their background and lived experiences, and their current circumstances. That said, be mindful of privacy and potential triggers. Some families may not be comfortable or willing to share all those details. And just as we highlighted the importance of building trust over time with students, we must do the same with families. If we want them to feel safe and have a sense of belonging, we should form a solid partnership between home, the school, and the community.

> "I think it's key not to work in isolation—it goes beyond building a relationship between the teacher and the student. Oftentimes, our information is very limited because the kids don't remember—you know, if they came from an orphanage or from a refugee camp—they just don't remember that experience. But there could be residuals from that—physical, mental, or emotional—that they bring with them that we have to try and figure out. And that can be very complicated. So I think the more people we have around the table, the better off we are. It takes a village."
>
> —District ELD Coordinator

To start, find out who is the first person in the school or district that will be welcoming and registering the students and their families, where this process takes place, and what steps are involved. If that is you, there are steps you can take to make that process as smooth and welcoming as possible.

> "The best way to let families know that they are welcome is to tell them."
>
> —Colorín Colorado (2018)

We know how important it is to reflect students' languages and cultures in the materials and resources throughout our classrooms. The same is true for our families. For example, our names are part of our identities. Pronouncing students' names correctly is important. We should also learn how to pronounce their families' names correctly—the first step in building that positive relationship. It is similarly critical to check that their names are spelled and entered correctly in the data systems and on any necessary paperwork or communication. Have a laminated card or reference guide for the front desk, for those who answer the phones, or for data entry personnel with phonetic pronunciation guides, as a reminder. The main office is an excellent place to reflect the languages and cultures of all families.

{ **Camila:** "For my family it was kind of hard. I didn't know English, they didn't know English, so nobody really knew English." Camila appreciated that some of her teachers were able to talk to her mom in Spanish at parent-teacher conferences so she could understand. }

We cannot underestimate the importance of communicating in the family's preferred language. A few strategies shared in Chapter 1, such as infographics, language boards/posters, and group holiday calendars can get you started. Remember to involve the entire school team—volunteers, support staff, office personnel, administrators, and so on.

## Multilingual Key Phrases

Display common phrases for greeting students and families, such as "*Welcome*" and "*How may I help you?*" in all the languages spoken by students and families. Other phrases might include "*Sign here, please,*" or "*Please have a seat.*" As you determine the most common phrases used, add those to the list. This shows that you care by taking the time to learn phrases in their preferred language and sends the message that you value their linguistic and cultural diversity.

## Infographics and/or Flags

These can be displayed in the classroom. Or you can create infographics about the countries represented by the families and students within the school. (See Who Are Our Newcomers?, page 9, for additional details on creating infographics.) Display them proudly at the entryway or in the front office. Another option is to display flags or images of flags from each of the families' countries of origin. This creates a welcoming environment for all.

## Travel Book

A travel book is handy as a reference for when new families arrive. If a family comes from a country that is not currently represented by visuals on the walls, or who speaks a language that is not translated on the language boards, pull out the travel book and have them show you where they are from as a starting point and opportunity for connection.

## Multilingual Staff

Determine who in the building and/or district is bilingual or multilingual. Create a list of staff members and volunteers, and the languages they speak, to use as a reference when new families arrive. Find out if there is a family liaison or family resource center within the school or district; this equips you with knowledge about who families can connect with for additional support.

## Reference Guides

Keep reference guides at the front office and for those who answer the phones. These can include the names of newcomer students and families with phonetic pronunciation guides, and even some common phrases, such as, "*How can I help you?*" in multiple languages. This will help ensure that students' and families' names are spelled and pronounced correctly by all staff and support newcomers' sense of belonging.

## Newcomer Kit for Families

In Chapter 3, we discussed newcomer kits for students. Why not have newcomer kits for families, too? The kits could include the following:

**Information card.** Provide a card with their name(s), language, address, and phone number, along with their children's names and dates of birth as a tool to use during registration.

**List of important contacts and information**. Have a list of important phone numbers and websites translated into all the languages represented. Add the school's website along with numbers for the front office, attendance office (if different), family liaison (if applicable), and community resources. Adding a school calendar and map would help, too.

**Information on how to navigate the school system**. Learning to navigate a new system is challenging. As one ELD teacher shared, "I think their biggest challenge is learning or relearning how to do school in America." Create short, translated videos that can provide valuable information on processes that are pertinent to the school. For example, what is the dress code or uniform policy? Where can they get uniforms? What is the grading system like? What do they do if their child is sick, late, or needs to leave for an appointment? It is fun to get students and community members involved in making the videos. They can even provide a tour of the school in their home language to share with their families. This does not have to come in the form of a video, though. Step-by-step written instructions for navigating the school system, translated of course, preferably with visual support, will be an essential resource.

**Adult English classes**. If parents and caregivers are new to the country and are interested in learning English, there are often opportunities within the community for adult English classes. Having information about available classes ready to share in their newcomer kit can get them started.

The more welcoming we can make our interactions with newcomer families, the more likely we are to foster positive home-school connections. Those initial interactions are critical. Greeting families with a kind, welcoming demeanor; using key phrases in their home language; displaying items related to their countries such as flags, infographics, and linguistic representations; and providing pertinent information in the form of a newcomer kit are the first steps in the process.

# Building Relationships and Communicating with Newcomer Families

Study after study shows that nearly all parents care about their children, want the best for their children, and want them to succeed (Epstein et al. 2019). In addition, research has shown most parents are eager to be partners with the school in educating their children (Epstein et al. 2019). However, when language barriers are present, family members may not get the information that they need to engage with the school to the extent that they would like.

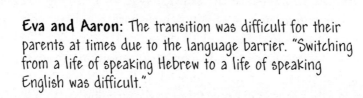

**Eva and Aaron:** The transition was difficult for their parents at times due to the language barrier. "Switching from a life of speaking Hebrew to a life of speaking English was difficult."

When families speak a language other than English, it can be intimidating for them to reach out and ask questions. So, how can we support them? Once you have established a welcoming environment within your buildings and classrooms, set up consistent systems of support and communication to build relationships. Below are some steps you can take.

### COMMUNICATE IN FAMILIES' PREFERRED LANGUAGES AND METHODS OF COMMUNICATION

The very first step in this process is to determine the families' preferred language and method of communication. The dominant language of the home is often identified via the home language survey (see Who Are

Our Newcomers?, pages 9–32). Many newcomers shared that additional communication in their home language would have been extremely helpful to their parents. So, let's make that happen. In addition, ask about their preferred method of communication. Do they prefer an email, a text, a call, a video, a newsletter, notes via Remind or Class Dojo, or hard copies of notes/papers sent home? What time of day might be best to reach them via phone? Then, when it comes time to communicate, do your best to honor those preferences. Ongoing, consistent communication has proven to make a positive impact on student learning and academic success (Epstein 2016).

"[The Immigrant and Refugee Center] has helped us with all of our parent communication, so that every time we send something out in English, it goes out in all the other languages, too. We do voice recordings in all different languages, being mindful of the fact that a lot of our families are not literate—just everything we can do to make sure our families have the information that they need. And, I mean, you can see it working because I just feel like our families before maybe were super nervous and uncomfortable about coming to school. Even today, when we were doing WIDA testing, families from all different places, they're getting comfortable just walking in and feel good about asking questions and they never worry about, 'Am I going to be understood?' And so that just feels like a win."

—District ELD Coordinator

## BILINGUAL RESOURCES

Consider having bilingual resources available to send home. These could include picture dictionaries, bilingual books, and passwords for apps and programs being used in the classroom (e.g., BrainPOP®, Reading A–Z®, Duolingo®). This provides access at home with their children, and sends the message that their home languages are valued and the maintenance of those home languages is encouraged. (See Who Are Our Newcomers?, page 9, or Resources, page 239, for more literacy resources.) Research shows that there are multiple benefits to bilingualism/multilingualism, and that language and literacy skills developed in the home language transfer and support the development of additional languages, such as English (Cummins 1981b).

## FIND POINTS OF CONNECTION

Hammond (2015) describes the importance of teachers finding points of connection with students. The same case can be made for finding points of connection with families. This could entail knowing a bit of their home language or enjoying the same sport or food, or maybe even sharing a connection of parenthood, if applicable. That way, you can start to build a relationship, which will serve to break down barriers and can increase their comfort level with the school in general and with communicating with office staff, teachers, or other education professionals in particular.

## HOME AND COMMUNITY VISITS

While sending emails, texts, and newsletters home can be quite effective, nothing can replace personal, one-on-one communication. When logistically possible, arrange to visit the homes and/or communities of your families (Colorín Colorado 2018). When arranging home visits, there are several elements to consider.

**Ask if visiting is okay.** We want families to know that this is voluntary and an opportunity to build that connection. We do not want to send a message that they are singled out or have done something wrong. Get families' consent, and then discuss location and scheduling.

**Determine a suitable location.** Some families may love having you over to their home, but it may make others uncomfortable. It is best to offer choices about where to meet, whether at their home or at a convenient location near their home. For example, the local library, community center, or park may be suitable alternatives.

**Set up a date and time.** Once you have agreed on a location, set up a time. Consider days and times that the parent or family member would be available. Sometimes this may involve evenings and/or weekends. Be flexible whenever possible.

**Go as a small team.** It is best to not conduct home visits alone. This is for the safety of the family and yourself. A great team consists of a teacher, administrator or other school personnel (e.g., counselor, family liaison), and an interpreter (if needed). More than two or three people conducting the visit could get overwhelming for the family.

**Start building the relationship.** During the visit, find points of connection with the family. For the duration, it is important to send the message that everyone is on the same team to support the student. Ask them what they would like you to know about their student. What goals or dreams do they have for them? What would they like their student's teacher(s) to know? Give them an opportunity to ask any questions they may have. Then, provide additional resources or information as appropriate.

### POSITIVE PHONE CALLS AND NOTES HOME

No parent wants to receive the dreaded phone call from school saying that their student did something wrong. Sometimes it is necessary. However, starting with the positive can set the tone from the beginning that everyone is on the same team to support the student and set them up for success. If you do not share a language, tap into other translation and/or interpretation resources. Is there a bilingual staff member who can help? In a pinch, there is always Google Translate, too.

## Bridging Home and School

Research shows that parents of diverse cultural and linguistic backgrounds are less involved in the school building unless the school organizes opportunities for families to become involved (Epstein et al. 2019). In some cases, due to work or familial obligations, it is challenging for family members to attend school events. We cannot assume that means they do not care.

**Casandra:** "It's not like they didn't care, they just didn't have the knowledge; especially of the United States. And they don't speak English."

The vast majority of parents *do* care deeply about their children's education, but may not know how to express that in a new language in a new country. How can we create such opportunities? Below are a few ideas for bridging home and school. Some of these are classroom-based and others are school-based. For the school-based activities or events, it is best to have an action team in place to support the efforts. It just takes one person to get the ball rolling, though. And that one person can be you!

## INVOLVE PARENTS IN INTERACTIVE HOMEWORK

Studies show that parents appreciate the efforts of teachers to inform them and involve them in their children's schoolwork and activities (Epstein 2016). Teachers play a critical role in the process of establishing a three-way partnership between themselves, students, and families. Researchers and teachers collaborated to create a teacher-parent partnership process known as Teachers Involve Parents in Schoolwork, or TIPS for short (Epstein 2016). These activities are created by the teacher for students to bring home and share with their parents or caregivers. The students become the teachers and "teach" their parents what they are learning in school. Then, the parent might be asked for input on a particular activity so they can be involved in a positive way. Students learn that it is important for them to have these conversations at home and that teachers want them and their families to talk about what is going on at school. There are multiple TIPS activities already created for literacy, mathematics, and science, grades K–3. The emphasis is on early literacy. However, many of these can be adapted for any grade level. Once you become familiar with the template and process, you can create TIPS activities for all grade levels and content areas. (See Resources, page 239, for access to the TIPS guide for teachers and other activities that have already been created.) Studies conducted on the incorporation of TIPS interactive homework show it has yielded multiple positive results such as higher grades, higher test scores, increased quality of writing, increased family engagement, and more positive school and family attitudes and emotions towards homework (Epstein and Van Voorhis 2001, 2012; Van Voorhis 2003, 2011a, b).

## STUDENT-CREATED VIDEOS

Students of all ages tend to enjoy using technology in the classroom. Find a way to engage them in learning opportunities while at the same time helping inform parents about the school—it is a win-win situation. There are many ways to get students involved by making videos in their home languages and in English. Providing information for families about the school has multiple benefits. Making videos is an opportunity to use and develop language. And since we encourage the maintenance of students' home languages, why not let them create videos in those home languages to share with parents? Then, they could create additional videos in English or watch other students' similar videos in English.

### Video Ideas

Here are some examples of videos that could be made and shared with parents.

**School tour.** Include the classroom(s), cafeteria, gymnasium, front office, and playground (if applicable). Enlist students to help—this would be a great *describing* activity.

**Daily schedule.** What does a typical day look like? Students create a video of their typical daily schedule. This would be a great *sequencing* activity.

**Same/different.** Students make videos about what they do in school and share how the activities are similar and/or different from school activities in their home countries. This could be a great *compare-and-contrast* activity.

**TIPS introduction video.** If you plan to incorporate TIPS interactive homework, which we highly recommend, part of the explanation portion could be done via video. There may be opportunities in class for students to make a quick video explaining what they are learning in mathematics, science, social studies, or language arts, or what they are doing in art, music, or P.E. Then, when interacting with the TIPS activities, they have a video tutorial to get them started.

## MULTILINGUAL/MULTICULTURAL SCHOOL EVENTS

Multilingual/multicultural school events (see below for examples) are a great way to bring families together. However, we must be mindful of barriers that may prevent family participation in school-based events. To maximize potential participation, consider ways to address the most common barriers of scheduling, transportation, and childcare. If you have asked families about their schedules, pick a day and time when most are available. If transportation is an issue, find out if there is money in the budget to provide it. And if not, is there a venue that might be closer to families' homes than the school is? If neither of those options is possible, consider carpooling or providing transportation volunteers. One of the best ways to address childcare is to allow parents to bring all their children. A creative, no-cost solution is to have local high school students volunteer to play games with the younger children in the gym. This has worked extremely well for many schools. It is important to get creative and think of ways to address the existing barriers.

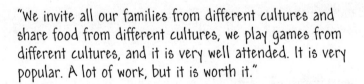

"We invite all our families from different cultures and share food from different cultures, we play games from different cultures, and it is very well attended. It is very popular. A lot of work, but it is worth it."

—District ELD Coordinator

## Ideas for Events

**Family literacy night.** Welcome all students and families to join. Have lots of books and other resources available in as many languages as you can. Students can read to parents or parents can read to students. Have an audiobook station as well for those who may enjoy sitting together and listening to someone else read a story. Encourage families to mingle. If appropriate and possible, provide some snacks and drinks to increase the enjoyment level. This kind of activity promotes language and literacy development and provides an opportunity for positive experiences for families at the school.

**International dinner and/or game night.** Food is often a way that people can connect and share a bit of their culture. Playing games gives families an opportunity to have fun at school as well as to connect. And why not sing some songs from other countries in different languages, too? The more we invite newcomer families to engage in enjoyable activities at the school, the more likely they are to feel welcome and that they belong.

**Cultural museum.** Have the students bring in something from their culture and work with the teacher to make a display. Students can then talk about what they contributed. This is something that could easily be expanded beyond the classroom to include families as well.

**Parent groups.** Do you have a high population of Spanish speakers, Arabic speakers, and/or Mandarin speakers? If so, creating a parent group based on shared language might be a possibility. For example, one school has a group called "Conexiones" for Spanish-speaking families. They bring food, have high school volunteers play games with the younger children in the gym, and bring in bilingual speakers on topics important to parents. They might bring in a speaker on mental health or a speaker to discuss how to help students use technology safely. There are always interpreters available and a variety of bilingual staff and community members. If you decide to start a group like Conexiones, keep in mind that these types of groups often start small. Then, if it is a positive experience, word of mouth tends to lead to increased attendance and participation over time. Persevere even if there is a low turnout the first few meetings. This provides not only a positive home-school-community connection, but it also provides a space for parents and family members to connect with one another and build a greater support network, which is extremely valuable, especially for newcomer families.

# Beyond the School: Community Resources and Partnerships

Most of what we have shared so far involves a heavy emphasis on the home-school partnership. However, it is important to note that there are often multiple resources beyond the school and within the community to support newcomer families. It is a shared endeavor. If you have a family liaison or a family resource center within your building or district, consider yourself fortunate, as that is not always the case. When researching what is available beyond the school, you might be surprised at what you discover. Take a tour through the area, either physically or virtually, to learn about the resources offered. Then, create a cheat sheet or community map listing all the resources to share with newcomer families as needed. Create a collection of pamphlets, too, that you can give to students or family members as appropriate. Look for the following resources for newcomer families.

**Family resource centers**. In some areas, there are family resource centers or even intercultural resource centers, often with bilingual staff or with access to interpretation services. These great starting points can connect families with the specific resources or support they need, such as food, clothing, shelter, medical care, and more.

**Refugee resettlement agencies**. Most of the larger cities in the U.S., and some of the smaller ones, have agencies that exist to support the resettlement of refugees, asylees, and other immigrant families. They offer support when people first arrive with housing, food, jobs, education, translation/interpretation services, English classes for adults, and other basic needs. To find the organization that supports refugees in your state, visit **acf.hhs.gov/orr/grant-funding/key-state-contacts**.

**Basic needs**. If your community does not have a family resource center or go-to organization, it is critical to know what *is* available to support basic needs in your area. Before anything else, a person's basic needs for food and shelter must be met (Maslow 1943). Do some investigating about the support(s) organizations offer, whether they have bilingual staff members, and how to go about accessing services. In some cases, certain services require documentation. Knowing this up front helps to equip families with as much information as possible to avoid frustration down the road.

**Bilingual counselors**. Mental health is of deep concern when it comes to newcomer students and families. Cristina shared that this was something she and her mom struggled with. They both felt like it was a good idea to talk to someone; not only because of the difficult transition, but because of what had happened in Colombia that they had not yet had a chance to "deal with." However, there was no one available who spoke Spanish. Cristina and her mom did their best with the English-speaking counselors, but ended up giving up after a couple of sessions due to the language barrier. These unresolved issues from Cristina's past continue to be a struggle. As Cristina explained, the challenge is "finding somebody that not only speaks your language, but that understands your culture."

**Military bases, universities, and faith-based organizations**. Sometimes we need to get creative when finding people in the community who speak the home languages of our newcomers. While the family resource center or refugee resettlement organization will be the best starting point, when those are not available, we are forced to think outside the box. Does your community have a military base or military academy? If so, do they host international officers? They may be a good resource. Those international officers likely have family members who came with them who may be looking for opportunities to connect with the community. Does your area have a college or university? If so, which language courses do they offer? The instructors and/or students might be interested in an authentic language exchange with newcomer students and their families. They could support newcomers with translating and/or interpreting, which would provide leadership opportunities and further community connections. How about faith-based organizations? Sometimes there are faith-based organizations that offer services for different language groups. Which ones can you find in your area?

**Community Services**

- food pantries
- shelters
- free or discounted clothing and/or hygiene items
- medical care (including vision and dental)
- mental health care
- foster youth support
- before- and after-school programs
- scholarships for youth sports and activities
- childcare
- programs to support LGBTQ+ youth
- transportation services (e.g., city bus passes)

**Note:** This is not an exhaustive list.

"I don't know how we would have been able to get through the pandemic without our partnership with the Immigrant and Refugee Center because they have helped us so much. We created 19 informational videos to help families understand quarantine and COVID. We [have topics] like, 'Your student needs to quarantine;' [Your student is] quarantined but they're not the person with COVID;' or, '. . . they are the person with COVID.' Or, 'Here is what happens when [school] goes remote.' So we have all of these instructional videos in all different languages."

—District ELD Coordinator

## Empowering Newcomer Families

We want newcomer students and families to feel welcome, connected, and supported. We also want them to have a voice. We want them to feel empowered to share their insights about their children's education to further strengthen those home-school partnerships. Whether they speak English fluently or do not speak a word of English, they should have the right to share their opinions, perspectives, and insights. We also want to tap into their strengths and assets to enrich the entire school community. Parents, especially newcomers, may not know the ways in which they can make their voices heard. It is up to us to tell them. Call them and personally ask them to contribute or communicate their ideas and opinions in their preferred language via their preferred method of communication. We need to inform them of these opportunities. Some of the below ideas likely already exist within your classroom or school. If so, it is a matter of encouraging their contributions. If not, maybe this will spark an interest in trying something new.

**Contribute to the class or school newsletter**. Most schools have some sort of newsletter, classroom-based or school-based. This is an excellent way to have parents' voices heard and deepen the representation of culturally and linguistically diverse families. They can share a quote, song, picture, story, or just about anything that represents them in some way. Have a family spotlight each week so students and families can get to know one another on a deeper level. This has the potential to lead to additional connections and networks of support, which is helpful for all families, but essential for newcomer families.

**Join a committee**. There are a variety of committees within the schools, such as the PTA (Parent-Teacher Association) or PTSA (Parent-Teacher-Student Association). Many newcomer families are intimidated by school to begin with, and the thought of joining a committee can feel overwhelming and out of reach. This is another instance when making a phone call or personally inviting them might result in a greater likelihood of participation. It is also necessary to have translation and/or interpretation services available so they can fully participate in the meetings.

**Start a group (e.g., Conexiones)**. This kind of group has the best chance of success when parents, as well as teachers and administrators, are involved. Ask them for guidance. Get their input and insights about how it could work. Ask them to share the topics they would like to discuss. Allow them to take the lead to the extent possible.

**Create opportunities for classroom participation**. Taking an assets-based approach to learning and home, school, and community partnerships, and capitalizing on families' strengths is key. Invite newcomer parents and family members to join the class when possible. Ask them to read a book to the group in their first language. Many books are translated into multiple languages. For example, the parent could read a book in Spanish and the teacher, or student, could read the book in English. Find out what newcomer families are interested in or passionate about; music, art, crafts, cooking, science, sports? When you see a connection to what you are doing in class, extend the invitation personally. For example, imagine you are reading a novel that is based in Guatemala, and you have a family from Guatemala, such as Casandra's. That could be an excellent opportunity to invite them in to talk a little bit about Guatemala. Or, if you are a P.E. teacher starting a unit on soccer and you know that one of your students' family members loves to play soccer, invite them to join in. The possibilities are endless. It takes getting to know your learners and families, finding those connections, and extending the invitations. Note: Each school has a different protocol for volunteers and visitors. Make sure you know the process so you, or someone in the office, can support the family in completing the necessary steps.

## Advocating for Newcomer Families

*Advocacy* is the "act or process of supporting a cause" (Merriam-Webster 2022a). Advocacy is associated with *action*. The *cause* is supporting newcomer families. Throughout this chapter, we have outlined several action steps that you can take to welcome, support, connect with, engage, and empower newcomer families. Successful advocacy is a shared, team effort. This involves the office staff, administrators, teachers, ELD professionals, and other school personnel. The goal is to create strong and positive partnerships between the school, the family, and the community. However, it starts with us.

Assemble an action team to create an action plan. Team-devised action plans allow for collaboration and give structure to the steps you can take to support newcomer families (Epstein et al. 2019). Begin by identifying your strengths. What are you already doing and doing well? Next identify areas of growth and even add in a new idea or two. While there are a multitude of ideas presented here, it is best to start small. Doing something is always better than doing nothing. Pick one area to focus on first. Then, focus on another. This is a process that takes time. However, the time is well worth it.

## Summary

We have taken a journey together throughout the last four chapters. First, you were introduced to the newcomer population—who they are, why they came, and how they came to the United States. After all, they are at the heart of all that we are talking about. Next, we shared some incredible stories of newcomers' experiences from their perspectives. The power of story is unmatched. The stories led us to consider the social and emotional needs of our newcomers first and foremost as some of them have experienced extensive trauma in their lives. In this chapter, we extended the conversation to include the families of newcomers and their communities.

Getting to know our learners and their families is an essential first step. Finding points of connection and building relationships built on trust is next. Without feeling safe and having a sense of belonging, academic success is nearly impossible. Now that we have considered the "heart" of our newcomers and families, we will move on to the "brain" and discuss supporting our newcomers' language and literacy development across the curriculum.

## Reflection Questions

- How have you or your school reached out to the families of newcomers? What are some ways they are welcomed into the school community?

- Do you think the parents and families at your school see themselves as partners in their students' education? Why or why not?

- What are you already doing to foster positive home, school, and community partnerships? What are some new ideas that you would like to incorporate?

# CHAPTER 5

# Designated English Language Development

## Language Acquisition

Supporting diverse English learners (sometimes referred to as *multilingual learners*) requires a comprehensive approach that includes both designated English language development (D-ELD): learning about English and its use, while putting it to use; and integrated English language development (I-ELD): accessing, interpreting, and producing language to succeed across the content areas in English. In this book, we define *designated English language development* as the dedicated time of day when students learn about the English language, the nuances of the language, and the grammar, usage, mechanics, and application of the language for a variety of purposes and audiences. What we refer to as D-ELD has also been called English as a Second Language, Focused Language Study, and English Language Development. We chose to use designated ELD because it emphasizes the need for students to have a specific time of the day that is *designated* specifically for English language instruction. The term was initially used in California's *English Language Arts/English Language Development Framework* (2015) as part of a comprehensive program for English learners. The framework states, "Designated ELD is provided by skilled teachers during a protected time during the regular school day. Teachers use the ELD Standards as the focal standards in ways that build into and from content instruction to develop the critical language needs for content learning in English" (31). Designated ELD should be just that: a protected time of the day, where students are grouped by English language development needs, to target English instruction. Differentiation goes deeper through D-ELD as students get their specific language needs met. This includes grade-level language needs that are drawn from content instruction as well as individual literacy needs. In contrast, during integrated English language development, students are in mixed-language groups in content-area classrooms. The support provided during I-ELD is differentiated for a range of language needs in the same class.

## What Is Designated ELD?

Newcomers come to school with very diverse academic and language experiences. These experiences provide the foundations, skills, and knowledge base ELs use to bridge their learning in and about English. The diversity of experiences means teaching and learning the English language is unique for each learner across and within grade levels. A student's English language proficiency level is not dependent on a grade level but on the language development of the child or adolescent when they entered into the new language. For example, a student may begin school in the United States as a ninth grader but with an early or beginning level of English language development. Another student entering the same grade level might have studied English as part of their schooling in their home country and so may be at a higher English language proficiency level. Therefore, focused language instruction needs to guide students in language development based on where they are in their English language development.

Integrated ELD targets grade-level language demands, while targeted language instruction focuses on language development levels. Collier's (1987) research focused on the number of years it takes English learners to develop academic English. She explained the need to understand students' language backgrounds to be able to estimate the time needed to reach high levels of English proficiency. Factors include the student's age upon arrival, English proficiency level upon arrival, primary language, basic math and literacy skills, and number of years of formal schooling. The varied language experiences of students reminds us of the importance of getting to know our English learners as individuals. All language variations, skills, and experiences serve as assets to draw from and build upon when learning a new language.

"Mohammed, who was from Senegal, joined my newcomer class at age 17. Omar, who was from El Salvador, joined my newcomer class at age 14 around the same time. Technically, Omar was a freshman and Mohammed a senior, but the class was based on English language proficiency level. And since neither of them had studied any English prior to their arrival, they both ended up in the same class. While their starting points were similar, their prior experiences were quite different. Mohammed had learned several other languages growing up in Senegal and was able to transfer those skills and acquire English more quickly. Omar, on the other hand, hadn't learned any other languages, besides his native language of Spanish, prior to coming to the United States. In addition, his formal schooling was interrupted, which meant he hadn't attended school in several years. He was catching up on content while learning English simultaneously, which was much more challenging.

To support the varying language backgrounds of my newcomer class, I provided lots of scaffolding in the form of visual support, sentence frames, vocabulary development, word work, attention to cognates, prefixes, suffixes, and so forth. The other thing that helped a lot was chunking. I broke everything down into manageable chunks based on their English proficiency levels at the time and prior learning. We did lots of hands-on activities, reading, and talking. Even though they had different starting points, they all made consistent progress over time."

—High School ELD Teacher

These varied experiences with language remind us to provide focused language instruction that meets each student's specific language needs. This instructional opportunity has an explicit focus on learning about the English language, including how to use language for a range of purposes.

California's 2015 landmark English Language Arts/English Language development framework showed for the first time the full integration of language and literacy. The framework reminded teachers that language and literacy are interrelated and part of all teaching and learning across disciplines. We use language to access, interpret, and produce thinking and learning. Historically, focused language instruction was taught in isolation from content-area instruction. Language was taught through isolated units or lessons that were helpful for teaching about language but did not address the intersection of language with the content students were studying. The California framework shifted how D-ELD was taught. The new focus is about teaching language *from* content. The core of D-ELD is still the language, but instead of taking an isolated language approach, explicit language is taught by looking at the language opportunities across content areas and using that content as the vehicle for teaching about the English language. Drawing from content makes learning about English meaningful; it gives language purpose.

**Camila:** "The hardest part for me was . . . my teacher had a small group of people that didn't speak English very well and she was teaching them. She had them at a little table. The rest of the class was doing assignments while we were in the little group. And she was teaching us how to speak English and it was more challenging with the homework because I didn't really understand it. I wasn't good at subtracting because I didn't know how to."

One thing that Camila's teacher did that made a difference was creating dual language cards. "So it was harder because she left me some homework that was in English, and I had to do little parts in English. And she also kind of helped me because she gave me a card that had *she, he, we, you,* and *I.* She gave me examples of what it was. And the back was Spanish so I knew what it was."

In many states, designated ELD is a required opportunity for English learners to receive explicit, targeted English language instruction at their proficiency level. Saunders, Goldenberg, and Marcelletti (2013) reviewed ELD programs and practices and found that successful programs do the following:

- develop English language skills in preparation for or related to academic content
- set goals and means for developing language as communication
- focus on language as the primary objective, with content as secondary
- emphasize language *in use* more than *knowledge about* language
- incorporate reading and writing, but emphasize listening and speaking

Designated English language development can be seen as its own content area, where ELD standards are used as the focus standards for teaching and students are learning about English in context. The dedicated time, coupled with students grouped by proficiency levels, allows for targeted language instruction. This further provides teachers the opportunity to use what they learn about students' past language and literacy experiences to bridge to English literacy. Regardless of grade level, students have targeted English literacy instruction to guide their overall language development.

During D-ELD, the focus is on developing the English language; therefore, students should be encouraged to speak in English. This is a time of day where English learners are grouped with students at similar levels and can feel safe and confident to try out language with others working together on similar goals. The use of the heritage language should be limited and used as a scaffold.

Students can use their heritage language to practice concepts or preview content that will guide their use of English. Figure 5.1 provides a brief overview of the key elements of designated ELD. English learners need time to practice using language at their level in settings that feel comfortable. Together in D-ELD they can take risks, make mistakes, learn from one another, and challenge their language skills. It can be intimidating for English learners who are newcomers to participate in English during their content-area classes, so D-ELD is a time of day where they can feel more comfortable practicing. For this reason, D-ELD time should provide many opportunities for students to communicate orally with one another to practice their English. In fact, many of the students interviewed expressed their gratitude for being required to speak in English, even if it was challenging at first. They recognized that they needed the practice.

Figure 5.1—Key Elements of Designated ELD

- It is a designated/protected time of the day for explicit English language instruction.
- Students are grouped by proficiency levels to address specific language needs.
- English is the language of instruction and should be used by students to practice language at their proficiency level. Heritage language support is used as a scaffold.
- Language foci are drawn from content instruction.
- It provides ample opportunities to communicate orally to develop language confidence and fluency.
- Explicit instruction of language targets includes demonstrations and modeling by teachers with opportunities for shared practice, leading toward independence.

## LANGUAGE PROFICIENCY

Designated English language development can best be accomplished when students are grouped by proficiency levels. Districts and schools use a wide range of indicators and descriptors to identify an English language learner's proficiency level. These descriptors demonstrate levels of proficiency that range from novice (emerging English language development levels), to intermediate (expanding language development), to bridging (reaching native-like proficiency) See figure 5.2 for a description of each proficiency level. As English language learners first come into a new language, they take time to understand the language, including its phonological patterns and meaning systems. They may exhibit a silent period where they are taking in the language and developing strong

**language targets**—language objectives; statements that describe how students will use language to demonstrate their learning

listening and comprehension skills. As their language comfort increases, they engage in the use of language for familiar purposes or for sharing new content expressed in simple sentences or other text-limited outputs. The development can happen quickly at first as students develop fluency of social English language skills, where they can reach an intermediate level of fluency. This conversational level of English demonstrates a sophisticated grasp of English and students can sound very fluent.

Figure 5.2—Language Proficiency Levels

| **Performance Definitions for the Levels of English Language Proficiency in Grades K–12** | |
|---|---|
| At the given level of English language proficiency, English language learners will process, understand, produce, or use: | |
| 6<br><br>Reaching | • specialized or technical language reflective of the content areas at grade level<br><br>• a variety of sentence lengths of varying linguistic complexity in extended oral or written discourse as required by the specified grade level<br><br>• oral or written communication in English comparable to English-proficient peers |
| 5<br><br>Bridging | • specialized or technical language of the content areas<br><br>• a variety of sentence lengths of varying linguistic complexity in extended oral or written discourse, including stories, essays, or reports<br><br>• oral or written language approaching comparability to that of English-proficient peers when presented with grade-level material |

*(Continued)*

123

Figure 5.2—Language Proficiency Levels (Continued)

| | |
|---|---|
| **4**<br><br>**Expanding** | • specific and some technical language of the content areas<br><br>• a variety of sentence lengths of varying linguistic complexity in oral discourse or multiple, related sentences, or paragraphs<br><br>• oral or written language with minimal phonological, syntactic, or semantic errors that do not impede the overall meaning of the communication when presented with oral or written connected discourse with sensory, graphic, or interactive support |
| **3**<br><br>**Developing** | • general and some specific language of the content areas<br><br>• expanded sentences in oral interaction or written paragraphs<br><br>• oral or written language with phonological, syntactic, or semantic errors that may impede the communication, but retain much of its meaning, when presented with oral or written, narrative, or expository descriptions with sensory, graphic, or interactive support |
| **2**<br><br>**Beginning** | • general language related to the content areas<br><br>• phrases or short sentences<br><br>• oral or written language with phonological, syntactic, or semantic errors that often impede the meaning of the communication when presented with one- to multiple-step commands, directions, questions, or a series of statements with sensory, graphic, or interactive support |
| **1**<br><br>**Entering** | • pictorial or graphic representation of the language of the content areas<br><br>• words, phrases, or chunks of language when presented with one-step commands, directions, WH-, choice, or yes/no questions, or statements with sensory, graphic, or interactive support<br><br>• oral language with phonological, syntactic, or semantic errors that often impede meaning when presented with basic oral commands, direct questions, or simple statements with sensory, graphic, or interactive support |

(WIDA 2007. Used with permission.)

## BASIC INTERPERSONAL COMMUNICATIVE SKILLS (BICS)

Jim Cummins (1981a, 2008) discusses the definition of Basic Interpersonal Communicative Skills (BICS) as the conversational, face-to-face, social language that students develop through engagement with and learning through a new language.

Cummins (1981a) found that BICS (the intermediate, conversational level of English) can be developed within one to three years. However, Cummins explains that the process and time to achieve fluency is not the same for all students. A range of factors impact students' language development

> **Basic Interpersonal Communicative Skills (BICS)**— language skills needed for everyday social interactions such as face-to-face conversations with friends, texting, and speaking on the phone

processes, including their age upon arrival, heritage language, foundations in literacy skills in their heritage language, and target language instruction in a home country. Newcomers are a very diverse group of students. We cannot make assumptions that all newcomers will take the same amount of time to develop BICS; neither will they all take the same amount of time to develop more academically contextualized language. It is possible for newcomers to arrive already speaking English and to enter schools in the United States at an intermediate level of fluency. Others might come from home countries where their heritage language was the only language accessible or used. For these newcomers, English is a new language when they enter schools in the United States. It is important in the process of getting to know students to understand their language backgrounds to best address their ongoing development during D-ELD.

## COGNITIVE ACADEMIC LANGUAGE PROFICIENCY (CALP)

As the language development process continues, students use English for a wide range of academic purposes. They build their knowledge of, access to, and use of language patterns for more diverse academic tasks. Students continue to develop language that is particular to a range of content areas and the academic language patterns that support the contextualized language of schools. Jim Cummins (1981a) called this contextualized, academic language *cognitive academic language proficiency* (CALP). This more expanded use of English can be seen as a bridging toward, or nearing, native-like fluency. When students reach this level of English proficiency, they may be ready for the reclassification process at their school sites.

The elementary and secondary education Every Student Succeeds Act (ESSA) of 2015 reminds us that even after a student has reclassified, they still need ongoing support for at least three years. This support can be accomplished through ongoing I-ELD.

reclassification—a process in which English learners demonstrate proficiency in district and/or state language expectations and are reclassified as English proficient

The range of listening, speaking, reading, and writing skills that contribute to fluency in academic language gives great purpose to D-ELD. Students at an emerging, novice level of English language development need different foci and support during D-ELD than students at intermediate or native-like fluency levels. The targeted support provided during D-ELD includes general language skills for a range of purposes as well as literacy skills. Designated ELD is the time of day when teachers cover language development standards and help students transition to or learn foundational English literacy skills.

The literacy development of students in their heritage language impacts how students gain English literacy. Depending on the language students come with, there may be parallels that can be explicitly built upon to help students bridge to English. Other languages that have different graphophonic systems (letter/sound correspondences) and orthographies (alphabets) need different support to bridge to English. For example, a student who has developed literacy skills in Spanish can be taught to draw parallels across the Spanish and English phonological systems, including similar letters, some with similar sounds, and others with unique sounds. This experience is different from that of a student who is bridging across languages with different orthographies such as the Japanese orthography and the English orthography. Such a student may need to learn the new English orthography more explicitly and directly because the same parallels cannot be made.

Even so, there are many transferable literacy skills and concepts we do not have to reteach. Students require help to learn the English language needed to express their thinking. For example, as part of literacy development, students learn how to compare and contrast as a core thinking skill. It does not matter the language they learn it in; the concept is transferable. If asked to compare and contrast in a language you are not familiar with, you could do it because you know how to compare and contrast. The skill is the same. How to *share* a comparison in a new language is the skill that needs to be taught. Teachers might support students with sentence frames for comparisons in the new language, which help them output the comparison. Second language acquisition research and theories support this transfer. Jim Cummins (2000) explains the common underlying proficiency theory that purports that the metacognitive knowledge and skills developed in one language help comprehension of and development of a new language. Understanding where students are in their literacy development in their heritage language gives us insights into the literacy skills they may have already learned, so we can help them bridge to expressing their learning in English.

> Understanding where students are in their literacy development in their heritage language gives us insights into the literacy skills they may have already learned, so we can help them bridge to expressing their learning in English.

Since many newcomer students do not come with records from their previous schools, having a heritage language assessment plan in place will be helpful for determining their levels of L1 language and literacy development. The availability of such resources varies from district to district. Typically, heritage language assessments are either designed locally or acquired from external providers. Locally created assessments are more cost effective but depend on having staff available who are proficient in the students' heritage languages. The use of externally created assessments depends on a district's budget. One organization that provides language assessments is the American Council on the Teaching of Foreign Languages (**www.actfl.org**). The ACTFL Assessment of Performance toward Proficiency in Languages (AAPPL) test is available for: Arabic, Chinese (Mandarin), English, French, German, Italian, Japanese, Korean, Portuguese, and Spanish. In addition, you can browse a database of language assessments by name of test, language, grade level(s), proficiency level(s), intended use, or targeted skill by visiting the Foreign Language Assessment Directory (FLAD) at the Center for Applied Linguistics (**webapp.cal.org/flad**).

## Scheduling Designated ELD

Learning about students is the first step in preparing for D-ELD. States are expected to monitor language development as part of the federal Every Student Succeeds Act. This requires an initial language assessment to determine a student's language proficiency level. Ongoing assessments that capture students' annual progress in language ensure that when students receive D-ELD, they are getting targeted instruction at their ongoing, developing language proficiency level.

Once student language levels are determined, schools decide how to group the students for D-ELD. This can be a challenge depending on the diversity of student populations and class schedules, making organizing for D-ELD a school-level discussion and decision. At the elementary level, schools may choose to have a specific time of day where the entire school mixes for D-ELD by grade level and students change classrooms based on their language development levels. For English-dominant students, this time of day can serve as targeted language study. All students need ongoing language development. Just as English learners are getting targeted language instruction, English-dominant students can engage in vocabulary expansion, creative writing, or other language areas of need.

However, this approach may be challenging in schools where the student population of English learners and English-dominant students is unbalanced. For example, if the school has 10 emerging, novice-level ELs, 50 intermediate-level ELs, 100 bridging ELs, and the remaining students are English dominant, then reorganizing students for D-ELD instruction might not work. The class sizes would be unbalanced. In these cases, schools have mixed ELD levels based on students' unique language development needs. You might have a student who is emerging but has developed strong conversational skills, so you might include them with the intermediate group. Or the students with bridging, native-like fluency might be joined by some English-dominant students. Other complexities may happen when schools have a very low number of ELs, where there are not enough students to form whole classes at any level. In

> **guided instruction**—an instructional practice in which the teacher uses appropriate scaffolds while students are engaged in productive group work with their peers (Fisher and Frey 2010)

these cases, teachers often have all the ELs in the same class and engage in small-group guided ELD instruction, similar to how small-group reading instruction works. Teachers have rotations for each ELD level to address the specific needs of each language group.

At the secondary level, the complexity of school schedules makes organizing for D-ELD a difficult but ongoing necessity. For ELs of all levels, D-ELD is needed and must be consistently provided because it is during D-ELD that individual language needs are met. What is important to consider when organizing for D-ELD at the secondary level is that students must receive targeted instruction based on their English language development level.

## NEWCOMER PROGRAMS

Secondary schools often provide designated ELD support through newcomer programs. These programs target the range of needs of newcomer students. A focus on their social-emotional needs and acculturation needs, as well as trauma-informed instructional strategies, is often included in such programs. The newcomers' needs are unique.

As an example, one school district in northern Colorado had a large influx of newcomers all at once. The district initially tried to have center-based support at the secondary level, designating one middle school and one high school to support newcomers. However, once the students exited the program about a year later, they had to choose whether to stay at that center-based school or return to their neighborhood school, which was often a different school. As the number of newcomers increased to about 80, the district realized they were not doing enough. The district sought funding to create newcomer programs at every middle and high school. They invested in teacher training related to English language development and trauma-informed practices, incorporated co-teaching, and found a solid curriculum that would work well for their students. The district ELD coordinator noted, "We have seen huge growth. Finally, we figured out what's best for our kids."

## WHAT TO TEACH DURING D-ELD

Designated English language development focuses on the language students need to engage with, understand, and use to successfully access, interpret, and produce language across content areas. Language instruction should be contextualized. The best approach is to look at how students are authentically using language across the curriculum. For example, if students are learning about historical figures in social studies, they are expected to understand and use the past tense. Teachers can then use this opportunity to have students learn about verb tenses during D-ELD. Drawing from language use in context can make D-ELD more meaningful. For secondary ELD teachers, it can help to collaborate with content-area teachers to understand the instructional pacing and standards of each content area so that ELD can be aligned appropriately. Taking time to review the standards for other content areas can also give insights into potential ELD lessons. These can include College and Career Ready mathematics and ELA standards, Next Generation Science Standards, history and social studies, even PE, visual and performing arts, and technical subjects. The point is to connect language to something familiar and authentic. D-ELD draws language opportunities from what students are already learning.

# How to Teach Language: Explicit Instruction

Saunders, Goldenberg, and Marcelletti (2013) suggest that explicit instruction is an effective pedagogical approach for English language development: "ELD instruction should explicitly teach forms of English (e.g., vocabulary, syntax, morphology, functions, and conventions)" (18). They further say that "ELD instruction should integrate meaning and communication to support explicit teaching of language" (20). The focus during D-ELD is on teaching the many and varied skills and concepts that help with listening, speaking, reading, and writing English and putting those skills into practice. When teaching these skills, it is helpful to use explicit instruction that provides a gradual release model. This coupled with the use of language for authentic purposes as the vehicle for communication can strengthen instruction during D-ELD.

> Language instruction should be contextualized. The best approach is to look at how students are authentically using language across the curriculum.

A pedagogical approach that supports explicit instruction is the gradual release of responsibility model (see figure 5.3). Fisher and Frey (2021) presented a framework that demonstrates the gradual release from teachers and carefully scaffolds instruction towards student independence. This model is often

referred to as, "I do, we do, you do together, you do alone." Earlier versions of this model did not include the "you do together" portion, but since then, research has demonstrated the importance of students working in collaboration as part of the scaffolding process.

Figure 5.3—Fisher and Frey Gradual Release Model

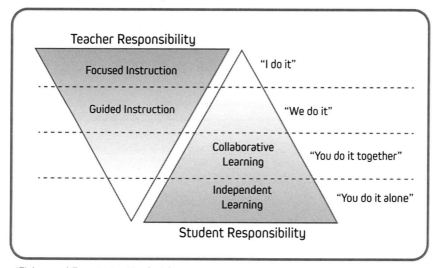

(Fisher and Frey 2021. Used with permission.)

Social Constructivism, a theoretical school of thought, reminds us of the importance of collaboration as part of the learning process. Seminal research by psychologist Lev Vygotsky (1978) presented the concept of the Zone of Proximal Development (ZPD), which explains that learning happens when students are supported to move from what they can do on their own toward learning targets through the support and scaffolding of a more knowledgeable other. Vygostky argues that learning cannot be separated from the social environment in which learning is occurring:

Every function in the child's cultural development appears twice: First, on the social level and, later on, on the individual level; first, between people (interpsychological) and then inside the child (intrapsychological). This applies equally to voluntary attention, to logical memory, and to the formation of concepts. All the higher functions originate as actual relationships between individuals (1978, 57).

Albert Bandura (1977) further expanded on social learning as part of his theory that emphasizes the importance of observation and practice through interactions with others. Baker et al. (2013) show that the explicit, direct instructional models of teaching, such as the gradual release model, have a positive impact on outcomes for students who struggle academically. Figure 5.4 provides an overview of the steps of the gradual release model with accommodations for newcomers. Figure 5.5 shows a sample lesson plan (on writing an opinion in a complete sentence) with noted accommodations for newcomers. Keep in mind that it may take several lessons to get through each stage of the model.

Figure 5.4—Gradual Release with Support for Newcomers

| Gradual Release Stage | Supports for All Students | Accommodations for Newcomers |
|---|---|---|
| Focused Instruction: "I do it." | • Teacher sets the learning target (presents the lesson objective) and demonstrates the skill explicitly.<br>• Teacher shows students *how* to do what is expected in the language objective. | • Teacher provides the objective in the students' heritage language(s).<br>• Teacher deconstructs the objective by highlighting cognates, providing images for key vocabulary in the objective.<br>• During the demonstration, teacher provides access through multi-cued, multi-modal methods (use of visuals, media, step-by-step demonstrations, clear language patterns accompanied with gestures as needed). |

Figure 5.4—Gradual Release with Support for Newcomers (Continued)

| | | |
|---|---|---|
| Guided Instruction: "We do it." | Teacher guides the students to practice the skill together as a whole group. | • Teacher presents the skill and content through multiple modalities.<br>• Teacher is mindful of students' comfort in sharing. (**Note:** If students are not ready to share out loud, cold-calling on students can be intimidating). |
| Collaborative Learning: "You do it together." | Teacher directs students to work with partners or in small groups to practice the skill together.<br><br>Teacher prompts and supports as needed when monitoring students. | • Teacher pairs students who share a common heritage language (if possible) for additional support.<br>• Teacher provides visual tools such as graphic organizers to guide the application of the skill.<br>• Teacher provides resources through different modalities to practice the skill.<br>• Teacher provides resources at different reading levels to practice the skill.<br>• Teacher provides sentence frames for students to complete written and oral tasks. |
| Independent Learning: "You do it alone." | Students practice the skill on their own. Teacher supports and monitors as students work independently. | • Teacher allows students to try out the skill in their heritage language as needed before asking them to demonstrate it in English.<br>• Teacher provides tools to guide language output, such as sentence frames, paragraph frames, and criteria charts.<br>• Teacher allows students to check their work with other students after they have had time to try out the skill alone.<br>• Teacher provides different options for presenting their learning, allowing for student choice. |

Figure 5.5—Sample Gradual Release Lesson for Expanding ELs

**Language Objective:** Students will write an opinion using complete sentences.

| Gradual Release | Lesson Design | Accommodations for Newcomers |
|---|---|---|
| Motivation | • Explain that students will practice using language to express an opinion.<br><br>• Define *opinion* as "how you feel about something."<br><br>• Present two pieces of fruit to the class and ask them to tell a partner which one they like better.<br><br>• Encourage them to explain why they feel that way. | • Choose fruits that are familiar to the class.<br><br>• Pair students by similar heritage language if possible. Allow them to share their opinion in their heritage language. (This is just a practice of the skill, so the language used at this point need not be English.) |
| Focused Instruction: "I do it." | • Tell students you will model how to express an opinion with three process steps: First, identify the qualities of the item; second, decide how you feel about each item; third, state your opinion and justify it by using the characteristics you identified earlier.<br><br>• Show two images of cars.<br><br>• Describe each image while pointing to it, and describe the different characteristics of each car.<br><br>• Write an opinion about which car you think is the best to take on a road trip and insert the characteristics you described earlier to justify your opinion.<br><br>• Reference the list of cue words to use when giving an opinion, such as *feel, believe, seems*. | • Demonstrate *how* to form an opinion and provide students with models of how to *express* an opinion, such as sentence frames and word banks with opinion cue words.<br><br>• Write the process steps on the board or on chart paper for students to access throughout the lesson.<br><br>• Interact with the list of cue words to show students how to use the provided tools.<br><br>• Use images to make the content easier to access, so the instructional focus is the skill of giving an opinion.<br><br>• Use relatable objects, such as cars, or familiar household objects, so students focus on the skill. |

Figure 5.5—Sample Gradual Release Lesson for Expanding ELs (Continued)

| Guided Instruction: "We do it." | • Tell students they will now go through the process steps with you.<br>• Play clips from two different songs, a slow song and a high-energy song.<br>• Ask students to share descriptions of each of the songs.<br>• Record their descriptions on a two-column chart to distinguish the difference between the slow and fast songs.<br>• Have students tell partners which song would be best at a sporting event, and have them explain why they think so. Remind them to use the descriptive words in their justifications. | • Use songs that are familiar to students, from different languages. Students do not need to know the lyrics to engage in the lesson.<br>• Provide sample descriptive words for songs, e.g., *slow, relaxing, fast-paced, loud, mellow, upbeat, energizing.*<br>• Allow students to share their opinions in their heritage language first if needed. Then encourage all students to practice sharing their opinions in English.<br>• Refer to the opinion sentence frames and remind students to use these sentence structures as they respond orally to you and to each other:<br><br>I believe _____ because _____.<br><br>In my opinion, _____ because _____. |

(Continued)

Figure 5.5—Sample Gradual Release Lesson for Expanding ELs (Continued)

| | | |
|---|---|---|
| Collaborative Learning: "You do it together." | • Tell students they will now practice with partners or small groups.<br><br>• Introduce a provocative topic as a prompt, such as "The principal wants to ban cell phones in school. Do you agree or disagree?" Remind students of the process steps, and that they need to justify their opinions.<br><br>• Have students discuss the prompt in small groups.<br><br>• Have each small group create two or three opinion sentences about whether they believe cell phones should be allowed in school. Remind them of the process steps, the word banks, and the sentence frames. | • Provide developmentally appropriate prompts. The focus is the *skill* of writing an opinion; the content is the vehicle that gives the skill context.<br><br>• If the topic uses complex language, students can preview the content in their heritage language, but the opinions should be crafted in English.<br><br>• Explain that, in this case, the characteristics they use will be justifications, or reasons that support their opinions.<br><br>• Provide additional sentence frames for giving an opinion:<br><br>  This is a good/bad idea because _____.<br><br>  Students should/should not be allowed because _____. |
| Independent Learning: "You do it alone." | • Provide students with images of different animals that have been kept as domesticated pets.<br><br>• Have students select two images and write two or three opinion sentences expressing which animal would be the best pet, and why.<br><br>• Ask students to read their sentences to partners to practice oral fluency. | • Use your knowledge of your own students to choose pictures of animals they have as pets, or other familiar animals from previous studies on ecosystems and living things.<br><br>• Students can first craft their opinion in their heritage language as they consider what they want to say.<br><br>• Return to the sentence frames used previously for support.<br><br>• If students continue to struggle with writing opinions in complete sentences, revisit the lesson later with the same focus, changing the content used to practice forming opinions. |

## Summary

Designated English language development is an essential part of a comprehensive program for English learners. During D-ELD, English learners receive targeted instruction at their English language proficiency level. Teachers provide explicit modeling of targeted language skills and concepts and allow students to practice using language with the support of their peers and ultimately on their own. Designated ELD should be coupled with integrated ELD that scaffolds instruction for ELs to help them access, interpret, and produce English to share what they have learned across content areas. Designated and integrated English language development are connected through rich content. In D-ELD, we can draw language targets from the content students are studying. The familiar context and content allow for the focus on language, so students are not overwhelmed trying to learn content and language simultaneously. They can draw from familiar content to learn language. Having a specific time of day where students are grouped by their English language proficiency levels provides opportunities to learn language within the students' language Zone of Proximal Development through the support of their teacher and peers.

## Reflection Questions

- How are students' language proficiency levels determined in your district?
- How do you differentiate for students with diverse proficiency levels?
- How does your school address D-ELD time, including schedules and instructional practices?

# CHAPTER 6

# Integrated English Language Development

## What Is Integrated ELD?

Integrated English language development (I-ELD) is a comprehensive approach to supporting English learners across the curriculum through intentional planning around the language demands of a lesson, providing access to the content, and allowing varied and ample opportunities to use language. Integrated ELD emphasizes the role of all teachers in the development of the academic language of English learners. Understanding the language demands across content areas will provide ELs access to the content and language of the discipline at hand and will also begin to show students that language is transferable. Making language explicit will help students "see" language and how many linguistic functions, forms, vocabulary, and discourse structures can be used to access and produce language across content areas. As part of this focus, students also understand how language has a unique role within a discipline, through discipline-specific vocabulary and common language functions, as well as how to extend the application of language across disciplines. Academic success for English learners requires more explicit English language instruction than what is taught as part of English language arts and English language development classes; it requires a consistent, multi-disciplinary approach. Newcomers especially need comprehensive support to connect their prior content learning and knowledge acquisition in a heritage language to learning in English across the curriculum. All teachers working with newcomers in any discipline can provide explicit and discipline-applicable support to foster academic language development.

Historically, I-ELD was referred to as Specially Designed Academic Instruction in English (SDAIE) or was part of Structured English Immersion (SEI) contexts. But in their original intent and implementation, both SDAIE and SEI only addressed strategies for making content comprehensible (input) as a key focus for supporting English learners across the curriculum. The focus on SDAIE strategies came out of SEI program approaches where ELs were expected to keep up with the core curriculum while learning English simultaneously. The intent was to provide a range of strategies that draw on multiple cues for accessing content. A key theoretical perspective in support of SDAIE strategies came from the work of Stephen Krashen and Tracy Terrell (1983) as part of their second language acquisition hypotheses—more specifically, the input comprehension hypothesis or comprehensible input hypothesis. This hypothesis posits that language learning experiences are enhanced when the message or content is comprehensible by the learner. If the "input"—what the learner is "receiving" or taking in—is comprehensible, they will have a better opportunity to access the content being transmitted through language and, in turn, develop language. Therefore, strategies shared with and used by content-area teachers focused on the input, making sure students understood what was being taught.

> All teachers working with newcomers in any discipline can provide explicit and discipline-applicable support to foster academic language development.

Integrated ELD builds on the work of SDAIE, showing that language is more complex and comprehensive. Students continue to need content to be comprehensible, but they also need opportunities to use language and engage with a mix of peers when discussing and producing language in all content areas. This comprehensive focus requires teachers to identify the language demands of their lessons, provide access to the content, engage students with the content through language opportunities (written and oral), and allow students multiple and varied opportunities to use the language for authentic exchanges.

The first step for content-area teachers is to understand their role as content-language teachers and to comprehend what is meant by I-ELD. They must see how it is different from focused language study (designated ELD). This knowledge is combined with an analysis of the role of language in their discipline-specific lessons, and a concrete definition of academic language. Once we can "see"

> Once we can "see" language in our disciplines, we can make instructional decisions about strategies to support the access, comprehension, and production of language.

language in our disciplines, we can make instructional decisions about strategies to support the access, comprehension, and production of language. Together, all teachers can support the language development of English learners for academic success.

## Designated Versus Integrated ELD

A comprehensive approach to supporting English learners is essential for academic success. Learning a language alone takes time. Learning content through the new language makes the experience more complex. English learners need opportunities to learn about the English language as part of explicit language instruction, and they need to learn how language works in context when learning across disciplines. The integral role of language in all content areas makes learning content while simultaneously learning language a challenge. While trying to access and follow along with complex content, newcomers are also trying to make meaning of the language patterns, vocabulary, syntax, discourse, and semantics of the language used to teach the content. Imagine a student taking a chemistry class in a new language: the student must follow the new language *and* learn the chemistry content of the lesson.

**Cristina:** Even though she was very athletic, Cristina said she almost failed P.E. in the United States. The transfer of skills was there, but the language barrier and the teachers' lack of training caused her to almost fail.

Remember, providing access to language is not reserved for the English language arts teacher and the English language development teacher. It is the responsibility of *all* teachers working with English learners. A team approach between language-specific teachers and content-area teachers, with the intention of supporting language across all disciplines will provide the necessary comprehensive support ELs need to succeed academically. This approach includes providing English learners with focused language instruction (D-ELD) and language support across content areas, including electives (I-ELD). There are many and varied ways of defining how we support language across the curriculum. This text uses the phrase *integrated ELD*, building upon the definitions set in the California ELA/ELD Framework (2015), because this term shows the relationship between language and content as symbiotic and not as separate areas of instruction. Using the term *integrated* calls out the focus of how language should be present explicitly in all learning experiences.

## A COMPREHENSIVE APPROACH

Providing English learners with D-ELD is one part of a comprehensive approach to their language education. While students receive targeted instruction, they also need support to access, interpret, and produce language based on what they are learning across content areas. Integrating language support in all content areas helps ELs engage with the grade-level content while continuing their language development. Throughout the day, English learners are mixed with peers at different language levels. Unlike during D-ELD, students access grade-level content and language regardless of their proficiency levels during I-ELD. Language is still scaffolded based on students' language proficiency levels, but the instructional objectives are based on grade-level content standards. Content is always primary in integrated ELD; language comes along the way.

**sheltered instruction**—a means for making content comprehensible for English learners while they are developing English proficiency (Echevarria, Vogt, and Short 2008)

Historically, I-ELD was discussed through the lens of strategies, such as SDAIE, ELD strategies, and sheltered approaches to teaching English learners. These approaches focused heavily on teachers making content comprehensible for students to maximize learning of the content (Mora-Flores 2018). While these strategies still support ELs, they do not provide an intentional and holistic approach to I-ELD. Integrated ELD includes making content comprehensible *while also* providing explicit language support, varied and frequent opportunities to use language to develop oral and written language skills, and analytic approaches to vocabulary instruction that show the transfer of language across disciplines.

> **Sofía:** Sofía's teacher helped her spell and pronounce words and learn sentences. One strategy Sofía found particularly helpful was seeing the sentences written on the board. Sofía also mentioned that having opportunities to talk to people in English in school and outside of school helped her learn English.

## Framework for Integrated ELD

Integrated English language development requires intentional planning to maximize language development opportunities within content instruction. It can be overwhelming to think about how language plays a role while already planning for rigorous content lessons. We present a framework for I-ELD (see figure 6.1) to guide teachers through key elements of this complex planning process. The framework includes focus areas that can optimize language support for all learners during content instruction and provide targeted support for newcomers. This framework was designed using more than 20 years of research and practice with K–12 teachers across the country, including analyses of reclassification data that showed how an explicit focus on language development across content areas provided strong opportunities for ELs to develop academic language (Mora-Flores 2018).

Figure 6.1—Integrated English Language Development: A Framework for Planning

- Set clear, deconstructed content objectives aligned to language objectives.
- Develop academic language.

    Identify the functions, forms, and vocabulary connected to the core learning objective.

    Promote vocabulary development by emphasizing the purpose of the words in context and use.

    Support language development through critical and creative thinking practices, including questioning practices.
- Provide comprehensible input so students can access content.
- Create opportunities for comprehensible output so students can demonstrate learning.

    Provide diverse opportunities to use written and oral language for a wide range of purposes and audiences.

**Eva:** One teacher "had her plan for the day and she knew that I was in her class, and she knew what language I spoke, so she translated all of her plan into Hebrew so I could read it every day."

## CONTENT OBJECTIVES

Learning is multifaceted. Every learning experience involves multiple skills, content, concepts, and language. Because of the complexity of any individual learning experience, it is helpful for students to know the focus of a particular lesson. Since there is always learning that happens beyond the objective, clearly stating the objective gives newcomers a sense of the intended outcome of the learning.

Objectives should always have four clear indicators of a learning target:

- content
- thinking skills
- resources
- products

## Content

The content is the "what" of the lesson. Which standard will this lesson address? In social studies, this might be "primary source documents." In English language arts, it may be "facts versus opinions." In mathematics, it could be "quadratic equations," and in science it could be "mitosis versus meiosis." In music, it might be "scales," and in P.E. it could be "calisthenics."

## Thinking Skills

A thinking skill indicates the cognitive enactment in which students will be engaged in order to master the content. In 1956, Benjamin Bloom, an American educational psychologist, presented seminal research to show the range of thinking skills from simple to complex, leading to mastery. Bloom's work was further developed by Anderson and Krathwohl (2001) to capture the active process of thinking, therefore turning the noun labels into verbs and adding additional layers of complexity. We chose this work to provide examples of a range of thinking skills that can be taught and scaffolded to guide the learning process. Skills range from simple to complex, and there can be more than one skill in a learning objective. All parts of an objective should be explicitly taught and be measurable. Be sure that if more than one thinking skill is included, each will be equally attended to in the lesson. Ultimately, what is important is that skills are present in the learning objective. Figure 6.2 provides a range of possible skills.

Figure 6.2—Thinking Skills from Simple to Complex

| Bloom (1956) | Anderson and Krathwohl (2001) | Actions or Activities |
|---|---|---|
| Knowledge—remembering or retrieving previously learned material | Remembering—recognizing or recalling knowledge from memory | • define<br>• identify<br>• know<br>• list<br>• memorize<br>• name<br>• recall |
| Comprehension—the ability to grasp or construct meaning from materials | Understanding—constructing meaning from different types of functions, be they graphic or written messages or activities | • discuss<br>• explain<br>• illustrate<br>• interpret<br>• restate |
| Application—the ability to use learned material or to implement material in new and concrete situations | Applying—carrying out or using a procedure through executing or implementing | • apply<br>• demonstrate<br>• dramatize<br>• illustrate<br>• interpret |
| Analysis—the ability to break down or distinguish the parts of material into its components | Analyzing—breaking material or concepts into parts, determining how the parts relate to one another or how they interrelate | • analyze<br>• categorize<br>• classify<br>• compare<br>• contrast<br>• differentiate<br>• discriminate |

Figure 6.2—Thinking Skills from Simple to Complex (Continued)

| Bloom (1956) | Anderson and Krathwohl (2001) | Actions or Activities |
|---|---|---|
| **Synthesis**—the ability to put parts together to form a coherent or unique new whole | **Evaluating**—making judgments based on criteria and standards through checking and critiquing | • compose<br>• create<br>• decide<br>• design<br>• evaluate<br>• produce |
| **Evaluation**—the ability to judge, check, and even critique the value of material for a given purpose | **Creating**—putting material together to form a coherent and functional whole | • appraise<br>• assess<br>• conclude<br>• criticize<br>• judge<br>• rate<br>• value |

Note, in figure 6.2, the change in the highest-level thinking skills, from *synthesis* and *evaluation* (Bloom 1956) to *evaluate* and *create* (Anderson and Krathwohl 2001). Also important to note is the change in the skill descriptions from nouns to verbs, suggesting these are actions taken by the learner, rather than static competencies. Figure 6.3 provides another visual of how Anderson and Krathwohl refined Bloom's work.

Figure 6.3—Bloom vs. Anderson/Krathwohl

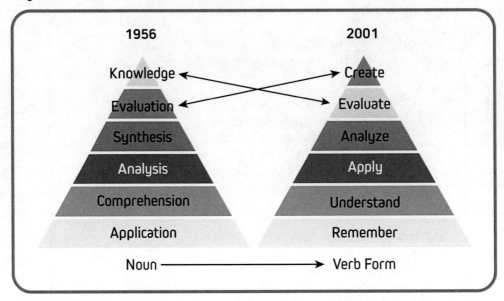

(Wilson 2001. Used with permission.)

In integrated ELD, content is key, but it cannot stand alone in a learning objective. We must be clear in what we are asking students to "do" during the lesson in order to master the content. For example, we would not want to say that students are going to learn about the rainforest without any indication of *how* they will learn about it. Objectives should include a cognitive enactment stating what students are expected to do or to learn about the rainforest. Do we want them to *identify* rainforests? Will they *compare* rainforests around the world? Will they be asked to *distinguish* predator and prey *relationships* within a rainforest? All content should be accompanied by at least one thinking skill. The "what" is the content, and the thinking skill tells "how" we want students to learn it. In some cases, such as in English language arts (ELA), the content might be the skill itself. For example, if the standard asks students to "compare and contrast," the skill is the same as the ELA content. In these cases, any subject matter or topic can be used to teach the skill. English language arts content often includes the skills as the "what" students are to learn. We also see creative skills in other content areas. For example, in science, the focus of a lesson might be to teach students how to write scientific reports, or in a visual arts class, the focus might be to create a model. Skills and content go hand in hand and together guide students through expected learning outcomes.

## Resources

Any specific content focus can be presented through a variety of resources. The internet has made resources more accessible for teachers. It is easy to find text sets, videos, pictures, lectures, books, oral readings of full texts, and a large variety of mixed media covering content across disciplines. Providing more than one resource during a lesson will improve your students' access to the content and skills. To best support newcomers, consider resources that are accessible to students with diverse language and cultural backgrounds.

## Products

The final component of the objective is products. We need to be able to assess to what extent the students met the objective. A product is a representation of learning and can include written, oral, demonstrative, or physical artifacts. Whenever possible, for newcomers especially, choice is important. The focus remains on the content, but students can demonstrate where they are in their learning through a range of products. As part of a study on describing animal habitats, the teacher might offer a choice board that includes a written paragraph, a diorama, a picture, a collage, a video clip, an oral presentation, a poster, and a graphic organizer (see figure 6.4).

Figure 6.4—Sample Choice Board

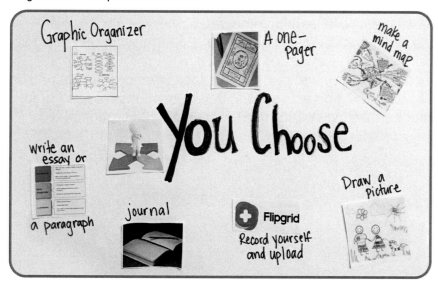

All of these products can demonstrate the students' learning, in this case, of describing habitats. Figure 6.5 provides a sampling of products students might enjoy across curricular areas.

Figure 6.5—Product Options

| Artistic/Visual Products | Performance/ Spoken Products | Written Products |
| --- | --- | --- |
| cartoons | advertisements | articles |
| charts | book talks | autobiographies |
| collages | dance | blog posts |
| diagrams | demonstrations | brochures |
| fashion design | poetry readings | comic strips |
| maps | readers theater | infographics |
| mobiles | singing | journals |
| murals | skits | minibooks |
| paintings | speeches | pamphlets |
| photography | tours | poetry |
| slide shows | videos | songs |

The four elements of a learning objective do not need to be in any particular order, but it should be clear for students what they are going to learn, how they are expected to learn it, what resources are available to them, and how they will demonstrate their learning. See figure 6.6 for examples of learning objectives for different content areas and grade levels that include a thinking skill, content, resources, and products.

Figure 6.6—Sample Objectives

**Science Content Objective, Grade 2**
Students will compare the predator and prey relationships across two ecosystems, using their textbook and online resources to complete a graphic organizer.

- **Content:** predator and prey relationships
- **Thinking Skills:** compare and contrast
- **Resources:** textbook, online resources
- **Products:** graphic organizer

**Health Content Objective, Grade 5**
Students will use a set of online resources to argue the importance of physical activity and engage in a class discussion.

- **Content:** importance of physical activity
- **Thinking Skills:** argue
- **Resources:** online resources
- **Products:** class discussion

**Mathematics Content Objective, Grade 8**
Students will orally retell with a partner the process of finding the $y$-intercept after watching a demonstration and completing a problem set.

- **Content:** $y$-intercept
- **Thinking Skills:** retell
- **Resources:** demonstration and problem sets
- **Products:** partner oral share

*(Continued)*

Figure 6.6—Sample Objectives (Continued)

**English Language Arts Content Objective, Grade 3–4**
Students will prove with evidence two character traits for the main character in *I Am René*, the Boy, and complete a labeled drawing.

- **Content:** character traits
- **Thinking Skills:** prove with evidence
- **Resources:** book
- **Products:** labeled drawing

## DECONSTRUCT THE OBJECTIVE

A comprehensive learning objective can be overwhelming for newcomers. A strategy that can help English learners when presenting an objective is to deconstruct it with them. Deconstructing a learning objective can help students focus on what they already know about the content at hand. Students can connect with the vocabulary or the thinking processes they are familiar with based on prior knowledge and language assets, such as cognates (words that sound similar and have similar meanings across languages, such as *music, musica, musique*). They will also be able to connect with their funds of knowledge that inform their learning experience. Figure 6.7 shows a deconstructed learning objective. Help students access the objective by reviewing it with them and making sure that any complex content or academic vocabulary is clearly defined or put into student-accessible language.

**deconstructed objective**—an objective that has been broken down into parts so that each part can be addressed

Figure 6.7—Sample Deconstructed Objective

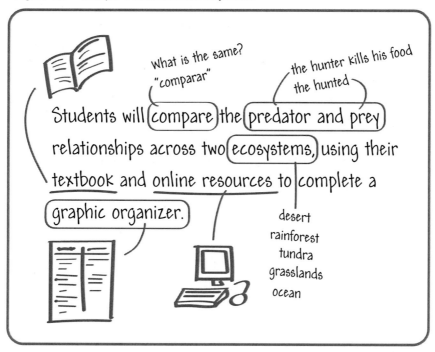

What is the same?
"comparar"

the hunter kills his food
the hunted

Students will compare the predator and prey relationships across two ecosystems, using their textbook and online resources to complete a graphic organizer.

desert
rainforest
tundra
grasslands
ocean

## LANGUAGE OBJECTIVES

In integrated ELD, the content objective will be the focus of the lesson, but language is part of all content instruction. The language development process involves the acquisition of language in rich contexts along with intentional language instruction (Cummins 1980; Krashen and Terrell 1983). A lesson that is accessible and purposeful, and that builds on prior experiences and funds of knowledge, will lead to language development. However, it is equally important to be intentional about what we expect of students in terms of academic language connected to the learning objective. For this reason, including a language objective connected to the content objective is an important part of I-ELD. When we create objectives, we not only hold students accountable for the learning, we hold ourselves as teachers accountable for ensuring that we are intentional and explicit in teaching to the objectives. A language objective can capture a targeted language skill or function, the purpose for using language, and sample language patterns or processes that students are expected to use. Kinsella and Singer (2011) offer a simple frame (see figure 6.8) for creating language objectives that includes an action verb (what we expect students to do with language) and then targeted language (what we expect them to use to meet the action verb).

Figure 6.8—Creating Language Objectives

Students will *(action verb)*, using *(language target)*.

OR

Using *(language target)*, students will *(action verb)*.

In I-ELD, the language objectives should clearly align with the content objectives so students can seamlessly meet both objectives within the same lesson. A teacher should not stop in the middle of a lesson to target a language objective; for example, talking about subject-verb agreement in the middle of a science lesson. However, the teacher might provide sentence frames and sample sentences to model language expectations that include proper subject-verb agreement. The language objective should be part of the regular processes students engage with to meet the content objective. Figure 6.9 shows how to align the sample content objectives presented previously with potential language objectives.

Figure 6.9—Aligning Language Objectives with Content Objectives

**Science Content Objective, Grade 2**
Students will compare the predator and prey relationships across two ecosystems, using their textbook and online resources to complete a graphic organizer.

**Language Objective**
Students will compare using compound sentences and comparative cue words (e.g., *similar*, *both*, *comparable*, *related*) orally and in writing.

- **Action Verb:** compare
- **Language Target(s):** write and orally construct compound sentences; use comparative cue words

**Health Content Objective, Grade 5**
Students will use a set of online resources to argue the importance of physical activity and engage in a class discussion.

**Language Objective**
Students will argue using present tense verbs (e.g., *contend*, *argue*, *support*, *believe*, *concur*, *disagree*, *agree*).

- **Action Verb:** argue
- **Language Target(s):** use present-tense words

Language objectives demonstrate how language is an integral part of every learning experience. At times, it is a challenge for content-area teachers to see how the development of language can become a normal process within the learning experience. However, content-area teachers play an important role in supporting newcomers through intentional language instruction embedded in content-area lessons. Understanding language connections can help this task feel less overwhelming. Be sure you are stating and implementing a language objective; making language functions, forms, and vocabulary available; scaffolding access to materials through images, graphic organizers, and multimedia; providing opportunities for students to talk with one another; and using a range of written tasks to practice writing about learning. We advocate for an understanding of how language is contextualized and how content areas create a context through which language is accessed, interpreted, and produced.

## Academic Language Development

The concept of academic language has been around for many years. More recently, there has been a push for academic language development as part of I-ELD. Many states have assessment measures that determine the level of English language development students need to "reclassify" or "exit out" of explicit support as language learners. Standards require that students demonstrate fluency in the use of academic English across all content areas.

We refer to *academic language* as the language that is contextualized to the purpose and setting in which it is being used; in this case, an academic setting and your classes. James Gee (2004) reminds us that all language is situational. This includes academic language—language that is used within the context of classrooms, across and within disciplinary subjects. A critique about the use of the term *academic language* is that it is often thought of as language that is more complex than what students bring to the classroom. All language is complex. The languages your students bring to your classroom from a variety of backgrounds—ethnic, social, sociocultural—are all just as complex as academic language. The communities in which the languages are being used include the same layers of language necessary for them to be a successful form of communication. These layers include an understanding of the phonology, syntax, semantics, and vocabulary of a language community. Ultimately, language is about communication. It is how members of a group engage with one another, transfer knowledge to one another, learn skills from one another, get basic and complex needs met, and capture their histories. The languages that students bring to the classroom, including different social constructs of a common language, can be seen as assets. Make connections between the context in which students use their home languages and the context of the classroom where they are expected to use academic language.

> We refer to *academic language* as the language that is contextualized to the purpose and setting in which it is being used; in this case, an academic setting and your classes.

We share this perspective because we believe in a culturally responsive approach to language development. To be culturally responsive means we value all languages, including heritage languages and any and all variations of English that come from the rich communities our students belong to. We do not believe that any one language is superior or should

> **asset-based environment**—an instructional approach that focuses on strengths, viewing diversity of thought, culture, and traits as positive assets; a classroom in which teachers and students are valued for what they bring rather than being characterized by what they may need to work on or what they lack

be valued more than others, rather we need to help students understand how language is contextual, and that all languages and their uses are equally important. Students will learn that school provides another context for language, and that is how we approach academic language. It is the contextualized language of school settings and the resources students are introduced to, interpret, and talk about in school. Students learn that there are specific structures, syntax, vocabulary, discourse, and semantics that are used in school settings, just as there are for language use in any and all contexts.

Academic language is sometimes referred to as the language of school, or the language of the disciplines. Flynt and Brozo (2008) add that academic language refers to word knowledge that makes it possible for students to engage with, produce, and talk about texts that are valued in school. It is also considered the "set of words, grammar, and organizational strategies used to describe complex ideas, higher-order thinking processes, and abstract concepts" (Zwiers 2008; 2014). Cummins (1980) argues that there is a difference between the language students bring from their social and familial language communities and the language that is expected in a school setting, where language is used to communicate thinking and learning. It involves a comprehensive understanding of language meaning, including the semantics, functions, pragmatics via analysis, synthesis, and evaluation of language in use.

The U.S. Department of Education published the *Newcomer Tool Kit* replete with an emphasis on the importance of explicitly teaching and reinforcing academic language for newcomers across all content areas. The tool kit presents the following principle:

> Instruction focuses on providing ELLs with opportunities to engage in discipline-specific practices, which are designed to build conceptual understanding and language competence in tandem. Learning is a social process that requires teachers to intentionally design learning opportunities that integrate reading, writing, speaking, and listening with the practices of each discipline. (2016, chapter 3, page 4)

The discussion of academic language as part of I-ELD is not new. The conversations, however, often speak in general terms, making it difficult for teachers to identify clearly what the academic language of their discipline actually *is*, beyond content-specific vocabulary. To help target and call out the language of the discipline, *academic language* refers to its functions, forms, vocabulary (content and academic), and discourse. The foundational work of Susana Dutro and Carrol Moran (2003) helps teachers identify the structures of language (the mortar) needed to guide students' thinking and the expression of language as well as the vocabulary words (the bricks) that bring their ideas to light.

## ACADEMIC LANGUAGE AS FUNCTIONS, FORMS, VOCABULARY, AND DISCOURSE

Every lesson you teach includes language. Students need language to access, interpret, and share what they are learning. Identifying the academic language students will need to help meet the learning targets for a lesson can help teachers be more explicit in providing and reinforcing academic language. *Academic language* as functions, forms, vocabulary (content and academic), and discourse are the structures of language that guide students' thinking. Figure 6.10 defines the components of academic language briefly, followed by a more comprehensive discussion and a tool that can support student access to academic language.

Figure 6.10—Components of Academic Language

| Function(s) | The purpose for using language |
|---|---|
| Forms | The syntax of language used for a common language function (purpose for using language); also referred to as *sentence frames*, *sentence stems*, the *mortar*, the *structures of language* |
| Discipline-Specific Vocabulary | Vocabulary frequently used in the context of a specific discipline, but used less frequently across academic contexts |
| Academic Vocabulary | Vocabulary that has high utility in exposure and use across disciplines and academic settings |
| Discourse | The structure of the interaction; can be written or oral |

### Functions and Forms

To identify the academic language used in a content area, start with the content objective. What are you asking students to do in their thinking? What will they be asked to learn? What are the thinking skills they will use? What we ask students to do to learn the content points to the language function. For example, if the content objective asks students to summarize a text, then the language function is "to summarize." The language function is directly connected to what students are expected to do cognitively. The thinking they are engaged in is what we expect to hear them express.

Once you have identified the language function, you can determine the forms used for that function. Use sentence frames or organizers to demonstrate how to translate the function into the appropriate form. Figure 6.11 shows examples of common language functions, along with possible forms that are used to express those functions, both orally and in writing.

Figure 6.11—Common Functions and Forms

| Functions | Possible Forms |
|---|---|
| argue | "One reason is _____" |
| | "I would argue _____" |
| | "Research shows _____" |
| cite | "As stated in _____" |
| | "From the text it can be determined _____" |
| | "The evidence shows _____" |
| compare and contrast | "While _____" |
| | "Although _____" |
| | "Similarly, _____" |
| | "Just as _____" |
| describe/ identify | "Notice how_____" |
| | "The picture shows _____" |
| | "The ___ looks/sounds/feels/acts_____" |
| prove | "For these reasons_____" |
| | "Therefore_____" |
| | "It is evident _____" |
| summarize | "In conclusion _____" |
| | "To sum up _____" |

## Vocabulary

Vocabulary for I-ELD can be specific to the content to be taught; it can also be academic vocabulary connected with the thinking skills used in a lesson. Academic vocabulary is distinguished from content- or discipline-specific vocabulary in that these words have high utility across disciplines. These words are conceptual and have high instructional potential, meaning we can teach about words with these words, including morphology, synonyms, antonyms, multiple meanings, and so on. Content- or discipline-specific vocabulary words will primarily be used in the context of the discipline. These words are considered low frequency because students will not hear or use them often outside of the content area. Figure 6.12 gives an example of academic versus discipline-specific vocabulary for the content area of science.

Figure 6.12—Academic Versus Discipline-Specific Vocabulary

| Topic: Cell Division | |
|---|---|
| Academic Vocabulary | Discipline-Specific Vocabulary |
| structure | meiosis |
| cell | mitosis |
| division | mitochondria |
| | metaphase |
| | anaphase |
| | prophase |

## Discourse

How will students be expected to represent their thinking? More than simply a sentence frame, discourse consists of language structures and generalizations based on specific criteria that are tied to the discourse structure. For example, a summary is a kind of text structure with certain criteria, whereas a presentation may have different criteria. A debate has structures and criteria as well, albeit represented orally. Whether students are practicing discourse in or out of the classroom, it is valuable and should be encouraged.

> **Mariama and Babacar:** Outside of school, Mariama had a job at Walmart. "I got to speak with customers, which helped me also with my English." Babacar worked at Walmart, too, and expressed that "working kind of helped because you have to speak to customers, especially working as a cashier in the front."

A Criteria-Language Chart is a tool to support discourse (see figure 6.13). The chart can include an outline or paragraph frame with language supports. Once the criteria are established, provide language supports that model the expectation. These scaffolds are not doing the work for the students; rather, they represent the expectation of academic rigor. A student can always go above and beyond the model you provide, but the model should set a grade-level standard. The components of a criteria-language chart are:

- **Discourse Criteria:** What is the structure of the interaction (oral or written)?

- **Language Supports:** What sentence frames, word banks, or other examples can serve as grade-level models for the student?

Together, the language function, forms (sentence frames), vocabulary (academic and discipline-specific), and discourse create an academic language bank. Figure 6.14 shows examples of academic language banks for two different objectives. Note that the sentence frames may also contain cue words to provide additional options and choices for students whose language proficiency is in the bridging range, and who may not require a sentence frame. Words like *difference*, *both*, *where*, and *however* may provide enough of a scaffold.

Figure 6.13—Criteria-Language Chart for an Expository Paragraph

# Expository Paragraph (Body)

| Elements | Language |
|---|---|
| **Establish Topic** | "First I want to talk about _____..." |
| •Who, what, where, how, why, or when. | "To begin with _____..." |
| •Establish sequence (first?, second?, last?) | cues: First, Second, Next |
| **Details describing topic** | — "Some people know that _____..." |
| •Facts about topic | — "According to _____..." |
| •Experience with topic | — "The text states _____..." |
| •Citing textual evidence | cues: text, reason, evidence, because |
| **Transition Sentence** | — "This is why _____..." |
| •Summarizing what the paragraph said about the topic. | — "Therefore, _____..." |
| | cues: (topic word), therefore, finally |

Figure 6.14—Academic Language Bank Examples

## Science Example

**Content Objective:** Compare the predator and prey relationships across two ecosystems to complete a graphic organizer.

**Language Objective:** Compare using compound sentences and comparative cue words (e.g., similar, both, comparable, related).

| Language Function | Language Forms/Sentence Frames |
|---|---|
| Compare and contrast | • "The **difference** between_____ and _____ is _____."<br>• "**Both**_____and_____are_____."<br>• "**Where**_____is___, _____is_____."<br>• "**The**_____is_____; **however,**_____ is_____." |

| Academic Vocabulary | Discipline-Specific Vocabulary |
|---|---|
| camouflage, capture, evade, protect | ecosystem, predator, prey, rainforest, tundra |

**Discourse Criteria**

Topic sentence

- Name the predators and prey
- Identify the ecosystems

Thesis

- State that either similarities or differences, or both, will be examined.

Supporting Evidence from the Text

- Quotes that show examples of the similarities and/or differences.
- Paraphrase the text and describe how the ecosystem influences the relationship.
- Provide a word bank of comparison words.

Concluding Sentence

- Restate the topic sentence in a different way.

**Language Supports for the Discourse Criteria**

Topic sentence examples:

- "In the ecosystem of_____, _____ is the predator that preys on _____."
- "The _____ and _____ ecosystems support the predator and prey relationship of _____ and _____ in very different ways."

Thesis examples:

- "The _____ ecosystem is a more _____ place for the _____ than _____ because _____."
- "Predators like _____ will thrive/struggle in the _____ ecosystem, because _____."

Supporting evidence examples:

- "In the text _____ shows _____."
- "On page ___, the text states, '_____.'"

Concluding statement examples:

- "It is clear that _____ was _____."
- "Therefore, based on the evidence from the text, _____."

Figure 6.14—Academic Language Bank Examples (Continued)

## Language Arts Example

**Content Objective:** Identify a character trait for the antagonist or the protagonist of the text and write a summary in your literary response journal.

**Language Objective:** Identify characters in writing, using simple to complex sentences.

**Language Functions:**

Identify

**Language Forms/Sentence Frames**

- "The _____ was_____ because_____."
- "The protagonist/antagonist of the story was _____ ."
- "He/She was a _____ person. For example_____."

**Academic Vocabulary**

summary, traits

**Discipline-Specific Vocabulary**

antagonist, character, protagonist, setting

**Discourse Criteria**

Summary paragraph includes...

Topic sentence

- Name the character
- Identify them as antagonist or protagonist

Thesis

- Identify the character trait for the chosen character

Supporting Evidence from the Text

- Quotes that show examples of the character's behaviors or actions that demonstrate the trait.
- Paraphrase the text and describe the character's actions and behaviors.
- Provide a word bank of possible character traits.

Concluding Sentence

- Restate the topic sentence in a different way.

**Language Supports for the Discourse Criteria**

(*Show examples of labeled antagonists and protagonists from previously read stories.*)

Topic sentence examples:

- "_____ was the _____ of the story."
- "The _____ of the story was _____."
- "The story had many characters, but the antagonist/protagonist was _____."

Thesis examples:

- "_____ was a _____ person."
- "Based on the text, _____ was seen as a _____ person."
- "I would argue that _____ was _____."

Supporting evidence examples:

- "In the text _____ this shows _____."
- "Throughout the story, _____."

Concluding statement examples:

- "It is clear that _____ was _____."
- "I can conclude based on the evidence from the text that _____."
- "_____ showed throughout the text that they were a _____ person."

This comprehensive tool makes explicit the academic language students will need to use to demonstrate they meet the learning objective. There is a significant amount of language in any lesson. An academic language bank provides the explicit language support students will need at a minimum to express their learning.

## Tips for Using Academic Language Banks

Here are suggestions to consider when using academic language banks:

- Provide a range of options for sentence frames. Students are at different levels of English language development and need access to diverse language options.

- Call out cue words in the sentence frames to offer greater support for advanced English learners who do not need a full sentence frame.

- Separate academic vocabulary words into their own list or highlight them in some way. For example, the words can be color-coded, or a star can be drawn next to them.

- Academic vocabulary can be used to make cross-subject connections. Ask, "Where else have you seen this word? Does it remind you of another word? What other words do we know that have similar meanings? What does this word mean in this context?"

- Discourse frames, such as longer paragraph frames, might reuse some of the sentence frames but reorganize them into specific language purposes or organizational structures. For example, sentence frames for comparison can be organized into a longer comparative paragraph (discourse) frame.

- Academic language banks are scaffolds. As students become more fluent, they may not need such heavy scaffolds.

An academic language bank is also used to explicitly show students that language is transferable. If they are asked to use similar language functions and discourse in other content areas, they can reuse the same parts of the language bank. The vocabulary may change based on the content, but the language structures and discourse are generalizable.

## Accessing Content Knowledge (Comprehensible Input)

For over 40 years, the research on supporting English learners focused closely on how to help students access the content. In the early 1980s, Stephen Krashen and Tracy Terrell introduced the idea of comprehensible input, which called upon teachers across content areas to understand their role in supporting English learners (Krashen 1981; Krashen and Terrell 1983). This idea states that if students are to learn content and develop the language connected to that content, the information presented must be comprehensible. If students are to learn and develop language, information must be presented in a way that is accessible, so students can make meaning from it and share what they have learned. Teachers rely on a variety of strategies and practices to support students' abilities to comprehend content, such as visual cues (e.g., facial expressions, gestures, images, drawings, graphic organizers, and demonstrations with realia) and auditory cues (e.g., expressive language, intentional tones, phrasing). Other strategies include activating prior knowledge, connecting to students' funds of knowledge, drawing from their home and community assets to help make content meaningful, using think-alouds to make thinking visible, and collaborative learning opportunities during which students learn from one another.

The strong focus on comprehensible input was furthered by the work of Genzuk (2003) and Echevarria, Vogt, and Short (2008), which focused on Specially Designed Academic Instruction in English (SDAIE). SDAIE incorporates a framework for thinking about how to make content comprehensible for English learners. To guide teachers in planning for SDAIE, Echevarria, Vogt, and Short (2008) created a series of tools that included the Sheltered Instruction Observation Protocol (SIOP). The SIOP model consists of eight interrelated components: lesson preparation, building background, comprehensible input, strategies, interaction, practice/application, lesson delivery, and review and assessment.

**Aaron and Eva:** "The only thing I wished in the beginning was to have a normal conversation with people, but I can't." Aaron said he communicated initially by pointing to things and using Google Translate. One thing that Aaron's teacher did that made a difference was that she helped his "brain to connect words with pictures." Eva agreed that showing pictures was really helpful. "That was a method I really liked."

**Sebastian:** Sebastian indicated that with respect to learning a new language, "it was probably the hardest and the best thing because you can use the new language to listen to music, make friends, and communicate with others." Speaking without being afraid of making mistakes and listening to music helped a lot. He indicated that it not only helped with learning the language, but with friendships, too.

**Gabriel:** Gabriel echoed Sebastian's thoughts about music. He mentioned the dual-language connection with music helped. "A lot of music that's popular in Mexico has both English and Spanish words . . . and you [understand], 'Oh so this means that and that means this.'"

**Mariama and Babacar:** For Mariama and Babacar, playing games was most effective. They had a chance to work together in a relaxed, fun way while learning English at the same time.

**Casandra:** Listening to recordings of songs in addition to hearing her teacher model language during reading and other activities helped Casandra with her pronunciation, which increased her confidence.

Supporting English learners to access content and develop skills while also supporting their access to academic language is necessary in all content areas. A multimodal, multi-cued learning experience should be part of students' learning throughout the day.

## MULTI-CUED APPROACH

A multi-cued approach requires thinking about the many ways in which students can access content. For newcomers, multi-cued access gives them a range of cues to draw on beyond auditory cues alone. Cummins (1980) talks about the challenges for students in schools when the content becomes very abstract. The visual and tangible cues that are accessible when the learning is concrete are less frequent. Cummins' notion of *cues* is reminiscent of *clues*. When teaching content, what are the different clues a student can draw upon to try to figure out the lesson at hand? The clues can come in many forms. They can include pictures, diagrams, cognates, labeling realia, and a variety of audible cues as well. These cues closely align to the SDAIE practices and strategies that focus on how to make content comprehensible for English learners.

**Casandra:** Casandra was helped by "big binders with a lot of stuff inside," morning warm-ups, writing exercises where they would "write five sentences about what you remember," group activities, making posters or drawing pictures and then explaining them (e.g., draw and describe your hometown), and class presentations. The teacher "made us do a lot of things to practice the English language."

**Sofía:** Teachers helped her spell and pronounce words and learn sentences. Seeing sentences written on the board was especially helpful. Also, having opportunities to talk to people in English in school and outside of school, such as ordering food, helped her learn English.

What makes teaching dynamic is the way teachers assess students' comprehension by watching and listening to how students make sense of the information. Assessment checks such as pair-shares, quick writes, table talks, and written and oral activities give teachers insights into how students are making sense of the information.

Teachers also read body language and facial cues when students are accessing the content to determine students' level of engagement and comprehension during instruction. As teachers watch and listen, they adjust and provide different cues. For example, teachers prepare visuals in advance and use tones, expressions, and intonations to make dynamic presentations. When students lose focus or seem not to understand the content, teachers adjust by reteaching or pointing out other clues from the text, the classroom, or tools they have used in the past. These are practices that make instruction multi-cued. We give students access to a range of clues or cues, and if they continue to struggle, we adjust and search for other cues that can further their learning.

When the COVID-19 pandemic began in the spring of 2020, teachers and students made a shift to distance learning. This added an extra layer of complexity to providing comprehensible input for students. Gone was the ease (for example) of having students engage in a pair-share while listening in to their conversations. Teachers lacked visual access to watch for body language. The multi-cued, on-site classroom environment in which students were previously immersed, where teachers could point to images and pictures or show charts and other tools to guide learning, was not easily accessible in the distance-learning environment. The challenge of bringing effective in-person practices to the distance-learning space initially inhibited support for ELs. Still, the concept of making instruction multi-cued was ever-present. Teachers began to explore ways to make the learning experience just as rich and comprehensive for students as in-person instruction. They used many strategies and tools:

- rich images and pictures from a variety of online sources
- online translation tools, providing students with access to audible versions of learning objectives and other content in their primary language

- synchronous meeting tools such as breakout groups, collaborative documents, and online polling and survey features
- videos from multiple online platforms, such as YouTube™ and Khan Academy™
- checks for understanding through written checks in a chat pod or brainstorming tools such as Jamboard™
- multiple opportunities for one-on-one discourse when students needed additional support

Students sent their teachers private chat messages if they were confused or needed help, they chatted with their peers to get additional support, and they met with teachers outside of class sessions to review any missed information. This range of comprehensible input practices that became common during distance learning can continue to offer students access to content during in-person instruction. Through learning management systems (e.g., Google Classroom™, Canvas), teachers can post resources and activities for students to work on outside of class.

> **Babacar:** It was helpful was when teachers would "stop and take the time needed to explain things." Babacar enjoyed discovering new ways of doing things, but also found the classes that were in English challenging. Having information online was helpful so he could take additional time later to better understand the content and material. The support of paraprofessionals was a big help, too. "We had someone there to explain everything once the teacher went over it."

## Multimodal Access

Couple a multi-cued approach with multimodal access to content to support English learners. To make content *multimodal* means providing students with access to content using multiple modalities. This could include the use of videos, online lectures, demonstrations, experiments, digital tools such as interactive games and activities, pictures, cartoons, texts, group work, and so on. During distance learning, multimodal learning became part of synchronous class time and was and can continue to be extended to asynchronous learning opportunities.

Many schools use learning management systems (LMS) such as Google Classroom or Canvas so students can access resources and tasks to be completed either in preparation for class or as extensions for homework. During the COVID-19 pandemic, learning management systems served as digital classrooms for teachers and students. On an LMS, teachers could post announcements or assignments, track student progress, provide feedback, grade assignments, email students, and provide a platform for collaborative learning experiences. This gave students ongoing access to the content. An LMS also archives student learning. Students could revisit content or review past lessons and activities so they could continue to learn on their own. The innovative practices and dedication to planning for multimodal and multi-cued learning experiences was inspiring during a very challenging time. The learning curve for teachers was extensive and teaching was exhausting, but the work has long-term impacts. The asynchronous materials that teachers learned about and used during distance learning can continue to be used to increase comprehensible input and language development for English learners during in-person instruction. The ongoing use of an LMS offers students access to content that can be accessed any time and reviewed as needed.

During distance learning, we revisited an effective practice for English learners called the Preview Review Method, which was introduced by David and Yvonne Freeman (2018). Using the Preview Review Method, English learners preview some of the language, content, or skills that will be taught, and are offered extended practices where they can review their learning. Figure 6.15 outlines an approach to planning for English learners that builds from the distance learning experience. An LMS can include asynchronous activities for students to review in preparation for class. During synchronous class time, students are with their teacher and classmates and can receive additional support to access and comprehend the content. After class, students have asynchronous opportunities to continue practicing what was learned.

With the focus of I-ELD being the content, asynchronous tasks before and after a lesson can include heritage language materials. We want students to build knowledge of the content, and that can happen in any language. Couple the heritage language support with English examples of the content to further guide English language development.

The use of an LMS makes this learning ongoing. The asynchronous tasks after class can include homework but could also include tools, resources, or experiences students can revisit to practice the language, access the content, and practice with the skills.

> **learning management system (LMS)—** software used to manage, document, and deliver classes and learning resources; learning management systems help monitor student participation and assess student performance

Figure 6.15—Plan for English Learners for In-Person or Distance Learning Environments

| Before | During | After |
|--------|--------|-------|
| **Asynchronous**<br><br>Multimodal opportunities in preparation for class<br><br>**Synchronous—** Extra support<br>• small group<br>• one on one | **Synchronous**<br>• clear objectives<br>• multimodal<br>• multi-cued<br>• oral engagement<br>• mental/physical engagement<br>• social development<br>• range of questions (analytic/ evaluative)<br>• explicit academic language | **Asynchronous**<br><br>Multimodal opportunities to practice and demonstrate learning<br><br>**Synchronous—**Extra support<br>• small group<br>• one on one |

(Mora-Flores 2020)

# Demonstrating Learning (Comprehensible Output)

In the early 1980s when the idea of comprehensible input was gaining traction and teachers were looking for ways to support English learners, another theoretical approach was introduced by Merrill Swain: the theory of comprehensible output (1985). Swain's work was not as well known or received because the focus in schools was on making content accessible to students. Output and use of language were included as comprehensible input strategies, intended to enhance comprehensible input. Swain reminded us that comprehension was not enough. If students are to become fluent in their ability to express their learning in oral and written forms, they need to engage in meaningful interactions that allow for feedback from a range of language users. This includes structured opportunities to use oral and written language for a variety of purposes, across disciplines. Dialogic experiences with language provide important opportunities for feedback. Students need to exchange language with the teacher and with one another. Through these exchanges students learn to correct their communication errors and change their language patterns, thus improving comprehension by the receiver. This stresses the importance of feedback on both oral and written language, especially because feedback on oral language is more immediate and frequent. Swain reminds us about the power of interaction and feedback to support language development. Intentional and frequent opportunities to use language across disciplines will enhance language development.

Students need to engage in meaningful oral and written interactions for a variety of purposes, across disciplines. For example, as part of a think-pair-share, students are asked to share their ideas with their neighbor. Often, though, they just state their idea, their partner tells them their own idea, and they are finished. Depending on the question or prompt, there may or may not be a back-and-forth exchange of language. During a paired discussion, however, a teacher poses a prompt or question and asks the students to each take a position and argue it with a peer. This requires students to go back and forth supporting their ideas, arguing their points of view, and providing feedback to their peers. Both of these paired exchanges are a wonderful way of engaging students in language with one another. What the paired discussion shows is more aligned to Swain's comprehensible output. When there is a back-and-forth exchange of language, there are opportunities for verbal and nonverbal feedback. A partner might ask, "What did you say or mean when you said . . . ?" Or a partner might make a confused expression. In both cases, this would require the speaker to fix up their language or give it another try. These ongoing attempts at language help with language development, as does the affirmation when a message is received and understood by their partner.

> **Julieta:** Not knowing the language was consistently reported as being one of the greatest challenges. Julieta shared an awkward moment during one of her first days at school. "My math teacher was calling roll and he went up to me and [said], '¿Cómo te llamas?'—what's your name? And me, not knowing what he said, I said, 'Gracias.' And the whole class just fell silent and were like, 'What? Her name is thank you?' I remember everybody from that day on knew me as the girl who doesn't know any Spanish at all." The struggles continued in geography class when her teacher didn't believe her when she told him that she didn't speak Spanish. "I tried to speak to him and just couldn't. And others in the class [said], 'Yeah, she doesn't know anything.' But he [said], 'Okay, read this paragraph in front of the entire class in Spanish,' so I did. And he [said], 'You're right, you don't understand Spanish.' That's what I said! And then everyone knew. It was super embarrassing."

The concept of comprehensible output reminds us that language development is not just repeating phrases or choral language rehearsals. It requires that students use language to exchange thinking around all kinds of content. Students should be discussing their learning in math and science, art and P.E., just as they do in English language arts and social studies. Discussing learning is not the same as just sharing the right answer, explaining a process, or retelling what the text or media source already interpreted and shared. Discussing learning requires students to exchange a broader range of ideas about what has been read, viewed, or learned. For example, in math, we want to ask questions beyond, "What is the answer?" There is not much to discuss in response to that. We should follow up with questions such as, "What would happen if . . . ?" or "Where could you use this math application?" The previous chapter discussed the importance of engaging students in a range of thinking skills and processes. This aligns directly with comprehensible output. If we limit thinking at the comprehension and recall level, students will use basic language patterns. If students are asked to analyze, interpret, critique, and create, they open up a broader range of thinking as well as opportunities to engage with their peers in discussions about their learning. We want to remember that our newcomers are a diverse group and we do not want to assume that they all are at emerging stages of language development or that they cannot process higher level thinking. All students are capable of higher level thinking, they just vary in how they are able to share, in English, what they are thinking and learning. We want to continue to ask a broad range of questions to challenge our students thinking in any language and to support ongoing English language development.

## Summary

Integrated ELD reminds us how a comprehensive approach to supporting English learners is necessary to achieve high outcomes in both content knowledge and language development. The foundations of I-ELD are not new. For decades teachers have worked hard to support students' access to their content. With students coming from such diverse backgrounds, the responsibility on the teacher is magnified. The work of I-ELD is the work of all content-area teachers. All disciplines are replete with language. Students must learn to access the content that is presented in contextualized language across disciplines. The consistency of language support and development across all content-area instruction will enhance the learning experiences of all students, but specifically newcomers. Feeling supported when moving across curricular areas helps newcomers feel valued and capable of academic success in all disciplines.

# Reflection Questions

- What is your understanding of I-ELD?

- What are the benefits of an explicit language objective in supporting language, especially for newcomers?

- What does academic language mean to you in your content area?

- What are some ways to make your lessons multi-cued and multimodal to increase access to the content?

- How can technology continue to support your newcomers, as well as all students, to access, interpret, and produce content?

- What opportunities for comprehensible output do you provide your newcomers?

# CHAPTER 7

# Language Input Strategies

## Strategies to Support Access to Content

Integrating language across the curriculum for newcomers involves a range of instructional strategies that can support students' access to content, help them interpret what they are learning, and produce language for a range of purposes, written and oral. Instructional strategies are scaffolds or supports that guide students toward meeting learning objectives. We implement strategies during lessons with the goal that students will learn to use them on their own when they need support to access content or share what they have learned. Students are introduced to a range of strategies that support content-area learning, as well as strategies that target students' language needs. The language development strategies work in tandem with content and other instructional strategies to meet the diverse needs of learners, including newcomers. Many strategies serve multiple purposes. They are selected based on student need and how well they provide support for academic success.

This chapter shares strategies to support newcomers in accessing content. The strategies are grounded in Krashen and Terrell's original work on the comprehensible input hypothesis (1983), focusing on the importance of understanding what is being learned. If we can understand the message, then learning can occur, and language develops simultaneously. The comprehensible input hypothesis is informed by Vygotsky's Zone of Proximal Development (ZPD): With the proper scaffolds and the help of a more knowledgeable other, students can learn. The i+1 and ZPD both start with learning about the student. What do they already know? What kind of schooling and/or experiences did newcomers have before coming to the U.S.? Then, build toward skills within the student's learning zone; those they can learn with additional support. Instructional strategies can serve as part of the supports, or scaffolds, that students need to help them learn. With a focus on input, text-based strategies are included to guide comprehension, listening and speaking, and vocabulary.

## Text-Based Strategies to Guide Comprehension

Students need help accessing content through different forms of text. Though there are various ways we can present content to students (videos, pictures, verbally, a demonstration, and so on), the following strategies are text-based. Many can also be used when scaffolding content presented through different media, but they originated from helping students with reading comprehension.

# Say/See-Mean-Matter

## What Is It?

This strategy helps students think about what they have read, viewed, or experienced by starting with the details and moving toward abstract concepts and themes. Students use a graphic organizer to capture what they extract from a text, what they think about it, and how it impacts their learning beyond the text. Moving students from the concrete to the abstract can help scaffold complex text or media.

## How to Do It

1. Select content that students need to process and analyze. This can be a traditional written text (informational or narrative); a media source such as a video, an image, a meme, or a political cartoon; or an experience such as a demonstration, experiment, or performance.

2. After reading or viewing the content, have students begin by thinking about the details or examples from the source. Using the Say/See-Mean-Matter template (figure 7.1), ask students to capture the details in the Say/See column. (The figure includes guidance on how to complete the template).

3. Ask students questions such as, "What did the text say?" "What did the video share about (topic)?" "What do you see in the image?" "What did they do in the performance?"

4. For the next column (Mean), ask students to consider what they read or saw and analyze it. Say, "Take a look at the details. What connections do you see? What do they mean?"

5. Guide students to look for patterns in the details, to consider what the author was trying to say through the details, and to explore multiple possibilities of the author or creator's thinking. Ask, "What is the main idea?" "What is the author's intent? "What message does the author want to convey?" Guide students to recognize the main idea or big idea.

6. When students provide a suggestion for the Mean column, ask follow-up questions to help ground their ideas in evidence, such as, "What made you think that?" "What from the Say/See column supports what you are sharing?" "How do you know that is what they meant? What evidence do you have?"

7. The final column is Matter. Ask students, "Why does this matter?" "Based on what we learned through the source, why does it matter to us? How does it impact our lives?"

8. Remind students that what we read and view in class is not just for class but connects to how we engage with the world around us.

Figure 7.1—Say/See-Mean-Matter Template and Guiding Questions

| Say/See | Mean | Matter |
|---|---|---|
| • Key details extracted from the source<br><br>• Examples drawn from the source<br><br>• Important information or facts from the source | • Look for patterns, key ideas, point of views.<br><br>• What did the author mean by . . . ?<br><br>• What did the author mean when they said . . . ?<br><br>• Why do you think they shared these details?<br><br>• What are they trying to teach us? | • How is this related to your own life?<br><br>• Why does this information or story matter to you?<br><br>• How does it impact your life?<br><br>• What connections can you make to your life? |

## Implementation Ideas

A traditional Say/See-Mean-Matter is simply the completion of the chart. Pushing it beyond the main idea and theme will help students develop stronger critical thinking skills and use diverse academic language.

• Challenge students to look for more patterns and relationships in the Mean column. Validate that all ideas are possible main ideas but use any similarities in student comments (such as words that are repeated) to determine patterns. The true main idea may be found in these patterns.

- Use the Matter column to help determine a theme. Themes are universal concepts that can transfer across settings, contexts, and disciplines, and are related to the world we live in. Ask students to again look for patterns or repeated words or ideas. Can they use one word or phrase to capture why all of it matters? For example, is it all about change, or relationships?

## Accommodations for Newcomers

Scaffolding from details to ideas to relevance helps guide comprehension. A few additional supports can further guide newcomers to engage in the strategy.

- Allow students to think on their own or collectively in any language that is comfortable and accessible to them and their peers. This allows the content to be processed prior to sharing what they learned and understood in English.

- Present the content through different modalities, such as text, videos, and images. A range of sources still supports the goal of the content and development of critical thinking skills.

- Allow for think-time. This strategy involves a lot of prompting. When asking a question, give students time to think before calling on someone to answer. As many newcomers noted, extra time was imperative.

- Oral rehearsals help with processing thinking and language. Students can talk about their ideas at every stage of the strategy with a peer or table group.

- Allow students to produce draft Say/See-Mean-Matter charts in their heritage language before transferring their ideas into English.

- Allow students to use bullet points with simple phrases or even one-word ideas.

- Provide a list of possible themes with cognates where applicable.

- Help students connect to the content based on who they are and their own experiences, to make it feel personal and inclusive to all learners from diverse backgrounds.

## A Final Thought

Say/See-Mean-Matter is a favorite among teachers during both designated and integrated English language development because of its flexibility. Use it in any content area, at any grade level, with any text type, and with varied sources of information (e.g., media, images, demonstrations, texts). It draws students in because they make real-world connections, which makes learning authentic.

# Main Idea Tree

## What Is It?

A Main Idea Tree shows students the intersection of topics, details, and ideas. When studying content, students often become engaged with details, soaking up all the interesting information. While the details are important, students should not lose sight of the main point or the main ideas of what they read. For example, students may remember details related to a war in history, such as specific dates or the names of a few battles. But thinking of why the war was fought will yield deeper understanding and help students remember the big ideas. Students should recall details, and push themselves to think about the why, the purpose, the point of view, the intent, and the ideas that can be taken away when the details work together.

## How to Do It

1. After reading an informational or expository text, do a quick check-in and ask students to orally recount what they remember about the text.

2. Ask students to share what the text was about to get at the topic. Decide if the topic is specific enough. For example, if the class read a text about the Roman Empire, and they describe the topic as "Rome" or "the Roman Empire," ask them to narrow their response to a precise chapter. Was it about all of Rome and everything related to the Roman Empire? Ask students to be more specific.

3. Once the topic has been identified, ask, "What point or argument is the author trying to make about (topic)?" or "What is the main idea or key learning or take-away that the author wants us to take with us about (topic)?" Continue to ask follow-up questions about the main idea.

4. Ask students to share evidence to support their main idea. Use a Main Idea Tree (figure 7.2) to capture their evidence. **Note:** Students may find more than three pieces of evidence. This example shows how to display the evidence as support for the main idea like the roots of a tree.

5. Use the Main Idea Tree as the framework for summarizing the text by crafting a simple paragraph using the notes from the tree. Model how to create the topic sentence by starting from the top of the tree. Use sentence frames as needed: "The text was about (topic)."

6. Think aloud as you use the main idea to create the thesis of the paragraph. Use frames such as "The main idea is _____."

7. Show how to use the details to complete the paragraph by crafting them into complete sentences to support the main idea. Use transition words or sequence words to connect the evidence.

8. Model how to combine all the sentences from the top to the bottom of the tree to create a summary paragraph.

Figure 7.2—Main Idea Tree

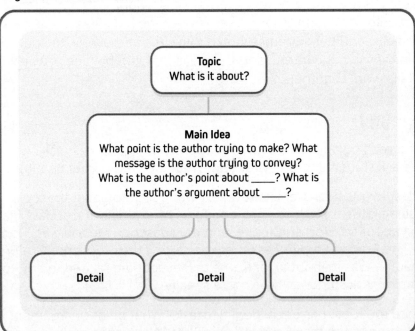

## Implementation Ideas

We spend time with the main idea when reading narratives because we think about the lesson or the moral, but the same must happen when studying all content. This strategy shows students the importance of capturing the topic and pushes them to think about the main idea.

- In mathematics, move beyond asking for the answer and how students solved it to asking, "What is it that this mathematical problem/concept helps us understand? What is the take-away? Is it that following a process can yield positive results?"

- In science, when studying plants and how they grow, push students to understand that the survival of plants relies on many external factors.

- In social studies, challenge students to go beyond memorizing facts and events to think about the effects of historical events on future events. How does the past shape our beliefs? Are there similarities to current events? Are there lessons to be learned from history?

## Accommodations for Newcomers

Newcomers are a diverse group and the accommodations here are not intended to demonstrate that they all have the same needs but to show additional scaffolds that can be used with the Main Idea Tree. The initial discussion is to extract details from the text. Here are some ways to scaffold even further.

- Capture the details on chart paper. Revisit the details and look for patterns: Are there words that repeat? Are there ideas that keep coming up? Circle or underline repetitive words and phrases. Explain to students that those words can give clues about the topic of the text.

- Use a Topic Tree to record the initial details (see figure 7.3). There may be more than three details. This example shows where to place the details on the tree. The Topic Tree goes above the Main Idea Tree to form a fully scaffolded Main Idea Tree.

- Once a topic is identified, have students practice saying the topic as a sentence to rehearse the writing to follow. Use sentence frames such as, "The text is about . . . ", "The book is about . . . ", or "The topic of the text is . . . "

- Have students discuss their thoughts about the main idea as a table group or with partners.

- Provide sentence frames for students to share the main idea with one another.

- Provide students with sticky notes and tell them to place the notes in the text where they find evidence to support the main idea. Ask students to share where they found evidence, what the evidence is, and how it supports the main idea.

- Provide a sample paragraph about a previously studied topic.
- Allow students to craft their ideas in their heritage language first if applicable, or to use pictures or storyboard applications. Then ask them to complete the paragraph in English.
- Chunk the text. Stop and complete a Main Idea Tree for every main heading if you're working with a longer text.

Figure 7.3—Topic Tree

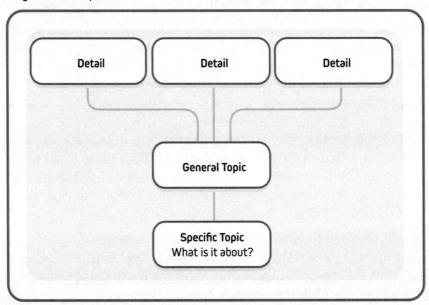

## A Final Thought

Guide students to provide more specifics about the topic. For example, if the text is about the fall of the Roman Empire, ask "What about Rome is addressed in the text? Does it teach about everything related to Rome? What specifically about Rome is the text referring to?" Once students can capture the specific topic, they can be guided toward the main idea by asking, "What is the author trying to argue or prove about Rome?" Too often students will name the topic as a main idea when a topic just captures "what the text is about" but not "what point or argument the author is sharing about the topic." Use guide questions such as "What is the author trying to teach you about (topic)?" "What point are they trying to make about (topic)?" "What are they trying to argue or prove about (topic)?"

## Language Input Strategies
# #Hashtag

## What Is It?

The #Hashtag strategy is used to chunk long pieces of text. As students progress in school, the texts they are asked to read become longer and more complex in terms of the amount of information shared, length of words and sentences, varied syntax patterns, discipline-specific vocabulary, and more abstract concepts. The #Hashtag strategy is a "during reading" strategy that asks students to pause along the way to think about what they have learned, to help track the content as well as their own thinking about it. Hashtags are used to capture and synthesize a topic or theme. When used online, they are a way of tagging content to cross-reference it, which can be brought into how students chunk text and process it one section or paragraph at a time.

## How to Do It

1. Introduce the text or content by reviewing the title or headers.

2. After reading a paragraph, pause and ask students, "How is the information being presented?" At this point, ask students to identify the text structure that was used to organize the information in the paragraph. For example, after reading a paragraph about using cell phones in school, pause and share that the structure was descriptive.

3. After identifying the text structure, ask the class to generate a possible #Hashtag to capture what that paragraph was about. If the article listed information about how students use cell phones in school, the students may decide on a #Hashtag called #SchoolUse.

4. Continue to read and have students pause after each paragraph to do a quick check-in about the text structure and a possible new #Hashtag.

# Implementation Ideas

Informational and expository texts have similar structures: description, sequence/time order/chronology, compare and contrast, cause and effect, problem/solution, proposition/support, inductive/deductive, and investigation. Figure 7.4 provides an overview of seven common text structures and keywords that provide clues to identifying them. Knowing text structures helps the reader see *how* the content is being presented to guide comprehension of the text. Connecting the #Hashtag with the text structures can guide students' cognitive process while they read complex texts.

Figure 7.4—Nonfiction Text Structures

| Nonfiction Text Structure | Description | Clue Words |
|---|---|---|
| Description | The text provides details or examples to describe the content. | • about<br>• has<br>• does<br>• shows<br>• for example<br><br>Look for: characteristics |
| Sequence/ Chronological | Information is presented in step-by-step order or follows a logical flow of time. | • first<br>• then<br>• next<br>• finally<br>• after<br>• last<br>• afterward<br>• later<br><br>Look for: times and dates |

*(Continued)*

Figure 7.4—Nonfiction Text Structures (Continued)

| Nonfiction Text Structure | Description | Clue Words | |
|---|---|---|---|
| Compare and Contrast | Similarities and/or differences are presented to show relationships within and across content. | • both<br>• alike<br>• unlike<br>• similar<br>• in contrast to<br>• whereas | • however<br>• in common<br>• as compared to<br>• different |
| Cause and Effect | The relationship between an event and what caused it to occur or the effects that occurred afterward. | • due to<br>• as a result<br>• because<br>• since | • cause<br>• effect<br>• result<br>• reason |
| Problem/ Solution | A problem or challenge is presented with solution(s) for addressing that problem. | • solution<br>• problem | • solved by<br>• decided |
| Proposition/ Support | A stance or point of view is presented on a topic, concept, or content with evidence to support the author's position or point of view. | • I believe<br>• based on<br>• it is clear<br>• proposition<br>• stance<br>• position | • because<br>• evidenced by<br>• based on<br>• clear that<br>• conclude |

(Continued)

Figure 7.4—Nonfiction Text Structures (Continued)

| Nonfiction Text Structure | Description | Clue Words | |
|---|---|---|---|
| Inductive/ Deductive | The information is presented from either part to whole (inductive) or whole to part (deductive). Content connects to a broader concept or big idea, or content is presented as a big idea with information about the parts. | • generalized<br>• concluded<br>• together<br>• deduce | • therefore<br>• in the past, therefore…<br>• theorize<br>• confirm |
| Investigation | The author guides or explains inquiry into some content or idea. | • research<br>• question<br>• considered<br>• wondered | • explored<br>• investigated<br>• observed |

## Accommodations for Newcomers

First, be sure newcomers understand the meaning of #Hashtag. We assume that everyone has access to the internet and cell phones, but that may not be the case for all newcomers. Be prepared to explain the strategy.

The #Hashtag strategy supports the needs of newcomers who can get overwhelmed with processing long stretches of content and, in turn, language. Chunking the text by paragraph helps break up the content and language. Newcomers process the text in smaller segments before moving on. When we read longer texts with students and wait until the end of the chapter or text to review what they learned, so much can get lost along the way. Comprehension is even more difficult when newcomers are working to understand the content and the language at the same time. Provide time for reflection and for processing the language to get to the content.

- Provide students with visible access to the text structure chart in figure 7.4. This can serve as a tool to comprehend the paragraph.

- Work with the students to come up with symbols or visuals that represent the text structure words. When students read, have them write the symbol in the margin identifying the text structure they think is being used. If students cannot write in the margins, provide sticky notes to draw the symbol on and place in the margin.

- Before agreeing on a #Hashtag, have students discuss options in their table groups.

- Ask students to write the #Hashtag in the margin or on a sticky note.

- Consider how much of the text to read before chunking. For advanced newcomer readers, go through more text before pausing to discuss and #Hashtag. The strategy is typically applied by paragraph, but as students become more fluent and comfortable reading longer texts, adjust how often you pause to accommodate developing literacy needs.

## A Final Thought

It is important to consider when any specific strategy might be needed. #Hashtag is helpful when students struggle to track comprehension while they read. If students seem to do well summarizing and comprehending text, they may not need a strategy like #Hashtag. Of course, classrooms are diverse in language and literacy needs. If one student needs more scaffolding and chunking than others, you could still use the strategy, but challenge the advanced readers to come up with more than one #Hashtag and debate which is best and why. This allows both struggling and advanced readers to benefit from the same strategy.

# Concept Blossom

## What Is It?

The strategies provided previously show the importance of deconstructing text by moving from the concrete to the abstract. The Concept Blossom strategy takes students beyond the text to connect their new learning to their own experiences and knowledge base. This increases the likelihood that students will remember what they have learned. In many classrooms, students regurgitate facts and details from a text or video but when asked later to recall their learning, they cannot seem to remember. The material was not relevant; it did not make sense to them. To remember information for the long term, students need to know how to make it personal. When students can make connections while learning, the potential for remembering is increased.

The Concept Blossom can be used before, during, or after a unit of study. Before a lesson, it is a way to activate prior knowledge and find out what students already know and understand about the content. During a lesson when some content has already been covered, or at the end of a lesson or unit of study, use it to recap or review.

## How to Do It

1. Select words from a broad range of topics or concepts connected to a unit of study. Write each word on its own sheet of chart paper.

2. Place the chart paper posters on walls or on students' desks. Have students work in groups of three or four. Each student will need a pencil or pen.

3. Have each group stand at one of the posters. Ask each member of the group to make a connection to the word written in the center of the chart paper. For example, if the word is *community*, each student should simultaneously write something that they can connect to the word, such as *neighborhood*, the name of their city, or *friends*.

4. Once the words have been written, they become part of the Concept Blossom. Now students can make connections to any words on

the chart paper. A student may branch out and connect a word to another student's word. In the example above, if one student wrote *neighborhood*, another student may make a new connection with *streets* or *trees*.

5. Once the new words are posted, those also become part of the Concept Blossom. Any word written is open for students to make connections.

6. After a few rounds, ask the groups to pause and talk about the connections they made. Each student should explain the different connections they made.

7. Ask each group to move on to the next poster and make connections. After all the groups have had the opportunity to go to the different posters, display them so they are visible to everyone.

8. Ask students to write the topic words in their notebooks and explain their personal understanding of them, including the connections they made and the relevance of these ideas. (See figures 7.5, 7.6, and 7.7 for examples of completed Concept Blossoms.)

Figure 7.5—Science Concept Blossom

Figure 7.6—Science Concept Blossom

## Implementation Ideas

- Use a Concept Blossom in mathematics. For example, during a middle school math lesson, students were discussing the constant of proportionality. As students tried to explain to one another what it meant, one student shared, "Think about when you're playing *Fortnite*. There is a constant of proportionality when you buy V-Bucks. But if you buy more at once then the constant changes." A group member replied, "Oh! That's what we have been doing? I mean, I was doing the problems all week. but I didn't know what it meant." Imagine this student playing *Fortnite* thereafter and every time she buys V-Bucks, she will be thinking about that constant of proportionality.

- Connect to students' heritage language (or languages). Figure 7.7 shows a Concept Blossom completed by newcomer students. One student wrote *enojado,* a Spanish word meaning "mad" or "angry" in English, as the connection to *fierce.* When asked about the connection, the student said they thought *fierce* meant "mad." These strategies are helpful because they can clarify misunderstandings. Another student explained that a lion is fierce, so they wrote the word *león* as their connection. After talking about lions being fierce, the group agreed that *fierce* did not mean "mean" or "angry." It was more about being tough or aggressive.

- Allow the students to make their own connections to help them better understand the content.

Figure 7.7—Concept Blossom by Newcomers

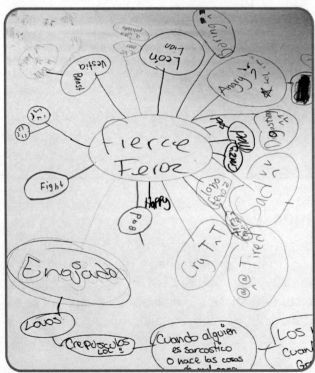

# Accommodations for Newcomers

The Concept Blossom is designed to help students make connections that draw from their own lived experiences and prior learning. This allows newcomers to make connections in any way that makes sense to them. Have students write connections in their heritage language when needed. The purpose is comprehension and learning, so the language they choose to write in can vary. As classmates interact, they hear from one another and learn about the content *and* the language. Students can draw pictures to make sense of the words in the middle, or translate the key words at the beginning. Some other accommodations for newcomers are listed below.

- Intentional pairing/grouping. Place students in mixed English language proficiency groups, but, when possible, try to have at least two group members who speak a similar heritage language.

- Add an image to accompany the starting words written on the chart paper.

- Encourage students to use words, pictures, or translations as needed.

- Have students talk about the connections they made before moving on to another poster to help practice language fluency and to help acquire language from one another.

- Have each group spend time on just one poster to present to the whole class. The presentation will serve as the vehicle for all students to learn about all the words. This allows newcomers to process only one term deeply, and then have peers make the other terms relevant and more accessible.

# A Final Thought

Students really enjoy Concept Blossoms because they make learning relevant. The connections are open-ended, so everyone can feel successful with the strategy.

# I Wonder

## What Is It?

A strategy that can be applied to any learning experience is to teach students to ask questions before, during, and after reading or viewing content. There are many, many questioning tools and processes that help students generate a wide range of questions about what they are learning. From Bloom's Taxonomy (1956) to Webb's Depth of Knowledge (2002), question stems and starters can be used to help students learn to craft questions. The I Wonder strategy keeps the questioning process simple. Students think about their learning at every step of the way through their own personal processing. Traditionally, students wait until the teacher asks a question to determine what or how to think about what they are learning. Teachers are wonderful at asking questions. Students expect teachers to ask the questions they want answered. The I Wonder strategy reminds us that learners need to become independent thinkers. We will not always be around to ask questions; students must be able to track their own learning. This strategy will seem very simple.

## How to Do It

1. Before beginning to read or view content, ask students questions such as these: "Look at the title. What does it make you wonder about?" "The video we are going to watch is about (topic). What does it make you wonder?" Have the students think on their own and write their responses in a notebook or share their wonderings with partners.

2. Ask a few students to share their wonderings with the whole class. If the sharing sparks answers or insights from other students, allow a brief discussion. Tell students to keep their wonderings in mind as they read to see if the text reveals new insights or answers.

3. As the students read or view the content, pause at logical stopping points and ask, "What are you wondering now?" Students can briefly share their wonderings with their tablemates or partners.

**4.** When the students reach the end of the text or video, ask them to recall what they learned, and ask one last time, "Based on all that you read and heard, what do you now wonder?" This will leave students with more questions about what they still want to learn and opens up the chance that they will continue to explore beyond the classroom.

## Implementation Ideas

- Predetermine stopping points in the text and have students read with partners to each point. When they reach a stopping point, have one partner ask a question, and the other partner try to answer it using evidence from the text. Then have them read to the next stopping point and switch roles. This encourages both partners to pay close attention by giving them each a purpose for reading.

- Have students record their wonderings on notecards. Collect the cards and redistribute them. Ask students to find the answers to the questions they were given.

## Accommodations for Newcomers

The I Wonder strategy is great for newcomers because it gives them processing time to think about their learning from beginning to end. Asking students to wonder validates that learning is complex and we need to stop and think. It is okay to not know something, it is okay to be confused, and it is okay to wonder what a word means. The I Wonder strategy shows newcomers that all students have questions, and questioning is a positive part of all learning experiences. Sometimes newcomers get nervous or are afraid to ask questions. Making questioning part of the learning experience helps students gain the confidence to share what they know and what they do not know. Additional accommodations for newcomers can include the following:

- Provide sentence frames for the wonderings. "I wonder . . . ", "I am not sure why . . . ", "Why did/does/do . . . ", "I am thinking, why . . . "

- When possible, pair each student with a tablemate who speaks their heritage language. Because the strategy is about comprehension, it is acceptable for students to process their thinking in any language. Once learned, conceptual understandings can transfer across languages.

- Allow students to share wonderings at any time. Students can be encouraged to raise their hands or use a class signal to indicate that they have a wondering they want to share. This might surface some needed language clarification.

- Consider when to chunk the text. Pause during narrative texts at significant plot or structure shifts. With informational text, use headings and subheadings to guide chunking the text. When showing videos, pause about every five minutes.

## A Final Thought

This strategy is a teacher favorite because it can be applied easily in any content area and with any text type or other media source. The ease of use makes the planning process manageable and the impact on students' comprehension powerful!

## Summary

Strategies bring lessons to life. Students become active learners when using a wide range of strategies because they are learning to problem solve when learning gets tough. There are many wonderful strategies that can be used to help students access text and increase comprehension. These strategies are favorites of ours and of the students and teachers we have worked with over the years. As we continue to engage with students, we recognize their varied language and academic needs and employ learned and new strategies that connect to those needs. When considering how to support your English learners, determine their needs and then make informed decisions about which strategies will work best, along with appropriate accommodations, scaffolds, and supports for newcomers. The strategies in this chapter can support that process. Use them when needed to scaffold access to text and improve student's comprehension of content and, in turn, help students develop language.

## Reflection Questions

- What are some strategies for comprehending and interpreting text you have found successful?
- How can these be modified for newcomers?
- What are some challenges when using these strategies?

# CHAPTER 8

# Language Output Strategies

The previous chapter on strategies for comprehensible input shared ideas for helping English learners access content by scaffolding reading and listening, with specific considerations for newcomers. The text-based strategies were comprehensive strategies that can be implemented during lessons when students need to comprehend and interpret text. In this chapter we present strategies for comprehensible output. There are many ways to support English learners in writing and speaking about their learning. We can scaffold written language by using graphic organizers, provide sentence frames, deconstruct writing, and allow for varied written products. Speaking strategies during lessons might include discussion structures, presentation guides, group and partnership work, and oral language rehearsals. In this chapter we present a unique set of strategies that are intended to provide daily fluency practices for English learners.

## Daily Language Practices

We present many different activities students can engage in to practice academic language. These strategies are sometimes known as bell ringers. They are short activities that are presented to students to complete as they are coming into class or settling in for the next lesson to begin. They are only about two or three minutes long, open-ended, low stakes, and connected to relevant or learned content. Mostly they provide a way to practice oral and written language.

These quick tasks are a great way to support language development for a variety of reasons. Most have no right or wrong answer; they just allow students to engage with content and explore language. They are designed to give students opportunities to practice language production at their own language development level. This way students at all levels can engage and still be successful within the intent and goal of the strategy. Newcomers especially can benefit from frequent use of short activities, because they allow time to play with language, apply language to content, and make mistakes with language to develop language fluency. The strategies can also be used as part of designated or integrated English language development. When used as part of I-ELD, include images or content connected to what you have been studying. For D-ELD, use any content or experience to draw from to practice language. To summarize, the strategies we have included are

- low stakes (lowers the affective filter)
- open-ended
- relevant, connected to familiar or prior learning
- opportunities for oral or written language practice at student's language development level
- quick (two to five minutes)
- a good way to increase daily language practice
- engaging

The strategies presented here can be used with all students; however, their nature can further support newcomers, as many are initiated with an image. This helps newcomers access the content they will write and talk about. The images you choose should depict objects or situations familiar to newcomers so they can draw on prior knowledge and experiences to practice using language.

Students can write their responses in a notebook or journal. The open-ended and individualized nature of the strategies should be honored. It is not necessary to provide sentence frames because the purpose is for students to develop their own language fluency and to see where they are in language. Allow students the freedom to just let language flow. They can track their progress by noticing how their language changes over time. This documentation of language production also provides an opportunity for a formative assessment of their language development.

# 10-Word Sentence Description

## What Is It?

The 10-Word Sentence Description pushes students to stretch out their language production. It challenges them to use more descriptive and complex sentences to describe an image you present. This strategy is intended to develop language fluency; therefore, be mindful that the content does not get in the way of practicing language.

## How to Do It

1. Begin by selecting an image. Choose from something that was already learned in class or an image that is relatable to students. Do not choose an image that is unfamiliar or that represents content that has not been covered.

2. After showing the image, ask students to write one sentence that includes at minimum of 10 words. Remind students there is no right or wrong answer and that if they are not able to reach 10 words, they should try to push themselves to add one more word than a previous attempt.

3. Once students write their sentences, have them share them orally with their table groups or partners. See pages 208–209 for examples of images used in K–12 classrooms.

Sample social-emotional image

Sample social-emotional image

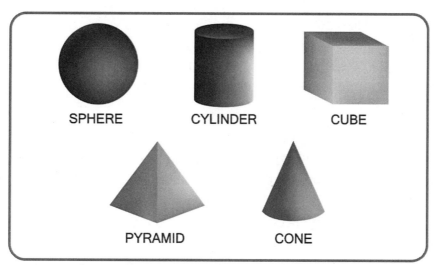

Image based on content previously taught

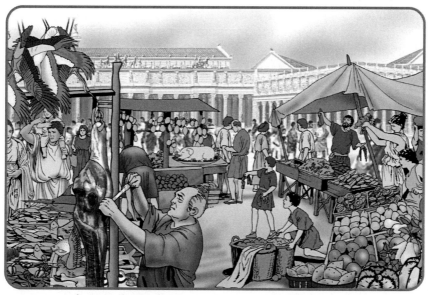

Image based on content previously taught

# Implementation Ideas

It is not the purpose of a 10-Word Sentence Description to get a correct response, and it is not necessary to correct students' sentences. However, you can share reminders to reinforce skills that you have been working on.

- For those students who may find 10 words easy, push them to use different types of descriptors or types of sentences.

- Reinforce writing techniques or grammar. For example, if the class has been working on prepositional phrases, ask students to each fit a prepositional phrase in their sentence.

- Address common syntax errors, such as, "Check yourselves, did you get to 10 today? Did you punctuate and start with a capital letter?"

- Ask students to include descriptors such as adjectives or adverbs.

# Accommodations for Newcomers

The 10-Word Sentence Description can also be differentiated for a broad range of language learners. The goal is for all students feel successful about where they are in their language development. As they record their responses throughout the year, they will see the growth. The strategy allows for students to work at their own level. If a student lists 10 words, that is a great foundation for writing longer sentences later. If a student writes a fragment, misspells words, or writes an incomplete sentence, the responses are all accepted.

- For those students who can only write five words, push them to add just one more, then one more again.

- Change the thinking skill to give students a broader range of language patterns to practice. Ask for a 10-word sentence explanation, a 10-word comparison, or a 10-word opinion. See the next page for examples.

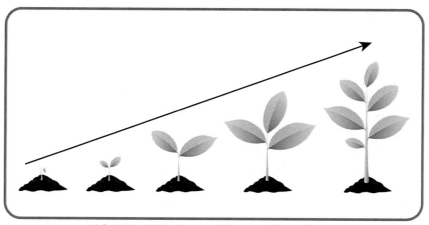

10-Word Sentence image for science

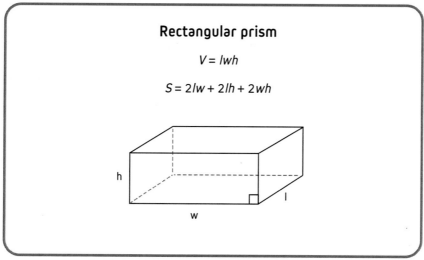

10-Word Sentence image for math

## A Final Thought

The 10-Word Sentence is a fun and challenging way to get students to engage in language production with their peers. Keep it fun, and make sure you are providing a safe environment in the classroom for students to take risks with language.

## Language Output Strategies

# Four Corners

## What Is It?

Like the 10-Word Sentence Description, Four Corners begins with images. Students are presented with several images and must explain how the images are related. There are no right or wrong answers. This exercise allows students to make connections based on their own prior knowledge, and to practice language discourse by explaining those connections.

## How To Do It

1. Present four images to students. These images should be familiar and based on previous learning or experiences or known content.

2. Once you show the students the images, ask them to share how the images are related. This is open-ended, and there are no right or wrong answers. Students do not have to write complete sentences—they are simply asked to document what they are thinking. (See below for an example of four images used in middle school D-ELD.)

3. Encourage students to share connections. Students may find commonalities, such as, "The images all show things people like to do." Students may categorize the images—for example, "The images all show hobbies." They are hobbies. Fun things. They all start with the letter C or are nouns. One student connected all the images into a story. "You put your hat on, get your dog in the car, and drive to the stadium to watch the team play."

Sample images used for middle school D-ELD

# Implementation Ideas

Intentionally select images that are related to a particular topic or unit of study.

- Encourage out-of-the-box thinking.
- Use Four Corners with different thinking skills, such as sequencing or compare and contrast. (See below for examples.)

Using Four Corners for sequencing

| A | B |
|---|---|
| $ac + bc = c(a + b)$ | $= \pi r2$<br><br>($\pi$ = 3.14 approximately) |
| C<br><br>= area of base x height<br><br>$= \pi \left(\frac{d}{2}\right)^2$ x h | D<br><br>$\frac{a}{b} + \frac{c}{d} = \frac{ad + bc}{bd}$ |

Using Four Corners to compare

## Accommodations for Newcomers

- Have students write their initial ideas in their notebooks and then share their ideas orally with partners or table groups. Or mix it up by having students talk first and then write down their ideas. Either way, students are writing and speaking each time they engage with the task.

- Ask for specificity, such as asking them to find a comparison, to create a sequence, or to create a story. Have them try out their ideas with partners.

## A Final Thought

Working with images bridges language proficiency levels and clarifies thinking for students. This activity encourages conversation and playfulness as students discover different relationships between diverse ideas. Sharing their thoughts lets them connect to and learn from their classmates in a non-threatening way.

# Snapshot

## What Is It?

Snapshot is a favorite language activity. Students are shown a small part an image and they must guess what the image shows based on the partial image. This activity encourages descriptive language and helps students learn to justify their predictions. Students will have a lot of fun trying to guess the image before it is revealed.

## How to Do It

1. Select an image that is familiar to the students. Show one small part of it to the class and ask them to guess what the full image is. Have them share their ideas with partners.

2. Show another, larger part of the image. Once again have students talk about their ideas with partners. Listen in as students engage with one another through oral language.

3. After two rounds, reveal the full image. Ask students to check their predictions. The images below show an example of a Snapshot progression.

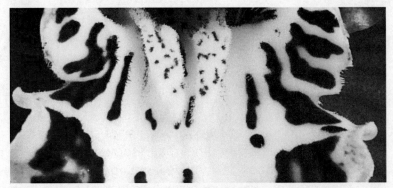

Snapshot Round 1

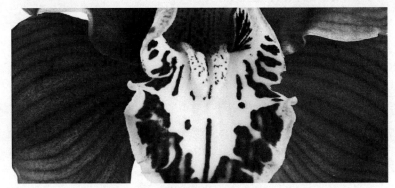

Snapshot Round 2

Final Reveal of the Image

# Implementation Ideas

This activity has a strong oral language component. The students' excitement while trying to guess the image is coupled with a natural back-and-forth exchange.

- Be intentional about the images you select. Choose images that are related to a topic or unit of study that you've covered to encourage incorporation of content-area vocabulary or concepts.
- Have students write their predictions in notebooks first. Ask them to justify their ideas when they share with partners. The oral language rehearsal is key to developing language fluency.

# Accommodations for Newcomers

Listen for rich descriptions as students try to help their peers see what they see. This leads to a robust exchange of descriptions and "Aha!" moments.

- Ask students to practice respectfully disagreeing with their peers or acknowledge if they are correct or incorrect.
- Encourage students as they use descriptive terms. Let them be creative and playful with the language they choose.

# A Final Thought

The oral language component of this activity is crucial for allowing students to experiment with description and explanation. Developing a comfort level with more varied terms (beyond *nice, small,* and so on) will serve newcomers when they need to use more specific descriptive words in their writing or speaking.

# Report It!

## What Is It?

Report It! asks students to use summative language patterns to tell the story behind an image. Use a familiar image, as the story is the goal. Students should not be wondering what they are looking at. They should feel intrigued to create a narrative about the image.

## How to Do It

1. Choose an image that is familiar to students or that was part of previously learned content.

2. Ask students to brainstorm answers to *who, what, when, where, why,* and *how* about the image. Tell them there are no right or wrong answers. They get to make up the story. Have students write their responses in notebooks. (Students do not have to write out their summaries, they only need to take initial notes on the *who, what, when, where, why,* and *how* so they can retell the story orally.)

3. Once students have taken notes, it is time to Report It! Each student will take turns with a partner or table group telling their own version of the story behind the image. Below is an example of an image and template used for fifth grade, along with a sample story.

**Extra! Extra! (Report It!)**

Who?
What?
Where?
When?
Why?
How?

"Chula, the neighbor's dog, was running across the park because he stole the big dog's bone. He dropped it way back because he was running so fast so he won't get bit by the big dog."

## Implementation Ideas

- Use this strategy to check for understanding. In language arts, show a picture of a character and have students tell the story of what is happening; in social studies, show a primary source document or a picture of an artifact.

- Narratives can be included in mathematics and science, with a little creativity. Ask students to tell the story of a triangle from the point of view of an angle, or have them tell a story about a science experiment using an element as the narrator.

- Ask students to keep their stories and revisit them to add more information or to turn them into longer narratives.

- Have students work in table groups of six. Place an image in the center of the table. Each student writes one sentence that answers *who* about the picture. Then, each student passes their paper to the student on their right, while taking the paper from the student on their left. They now must add a sentence about the *what* of the picture, working off of the first sentence. In effect, they are each contributing one line to a story that is being built collaboratively. Have students continue until all the questions have been answered. The story now goes back to the student who wrote the first sentence. Each student shares their finished story, and the group discusses the different progressions of the stories.

## Accommodations for Newcomers

- Provide a template with each of the *W* words to prompt students as they jot down their notes. Consider using heritage languages as well.
- Use color coding to identify the question word and ask partners to identify which question words were addressed in the story.

## A Final Thought

Look for images for this exercise that are intriguing, that elicit an emotional response, or that are unusual. Also, consider images from around the world so newcomers see images that may be familiar to them. These types of images will prove more interesting and will inspire rich descriptions and imaginative responses.

# Where in the World?

## What Is It?

Where in the World? asks students to place an image or an artifact in a location or to imagine how it fits into their own lives. This activity can help students connect content to their experiences to add relevancy to what they are learning. Students get to share their unique background knowledge, which will help newcomers get to know others in the class.

## How to Do It

1. Show the class an image or interesting artifact.

2. Ask, "Where in the world would you see this? Why do you think so?"

3. Have students share their ideas with partners, and then share with the class. There are no right or wrong answers. Allow language to flow and personal ideas to be explored.

## Implementation Ideas

Students will enjoy thinking about how they can picture the item or image in their own lives. You may also select an image that some students might know only in their imaginations, such as the one shown below. Sample student responses to that image included: "I have seen that when I went camping with my family;" "We have something like that in Guadalajara where we walk;" "I saw it in an ad for planes;" "I can see it in the forest so I can swim there."

- The image or item should be interesting and can be pulled from previously studied content to allow students time to explore its relevance in their lives. For example, show images from ancient civilizations in history, a phenomenon from science, or a math-related image such as the Great Pyramids of Egypt.

- Turn this exercise into What in the World? by showing an object that is from another time period or one that is related to something the students might not know, such as an unusual tool or device. Have them describe what they are seeing and explain how it might be used.

- Use discipline-specific vocabulary words and corresponding pictures to explore how students are seeing the relevance of the words beyond the classroom.

- Ask students to think of more than one application in the real world.

Sample image for Where in the World?

## Accommodations for Newcomers

- Ask students to share their ideas with partners first. Have students work together to construct a description of where they think the image or item would be found.

- Extend the lesson if students show interest in a particular image. Ask students to research the item or image.

## A Final Thought

Use What in the World? to foster an asset-based environment by honoring items and images that represent different cultures, countries, and ethnicities.

# Which Three Do You See?

## What Is It?

The use of images in the previous activities provides visual support, helping newcomers feel welcomed into the activity. This activity is a little more complicated because it begins with text, through a word search. There are many online tools for creating original word searches, such as **puzzlemaker.discoveryeducation.com/word-search**. The key is for you to create them so they connect with your students.

## How to Do It

1. Provide students with a word search.

2. Give students a short amount of time to look at the word search and write down the first three words they see. Have them share their words orally with a partner.

3. Have each student write a sentence that contains all three words. The sentences should not be corrected for grammar or spelling so that students have fun with language and feel comfortable crafting their own original sentences.

4. Ask students to share their sentences with partners.

## Implementation Ideas

- Select more than three words to challenge those who are ready to create longer sentences.

- Ask students to explain a connection between the three words. Have them write a short paragraph that uses all three words.

- Have students create clues for their three words and use a puzzle maker site to create crosswords. Each week, offer a new puzzle for the class to solve.

## Accommodations for Newcomers

- If students need support finding words, circle a range of words and ask them to choose from those circled.

- Select only two words at first for students who are at emerging stages of language development.

- Include words that are familiar to students or use vocabulary they have studied. This allows students to see some familiar words and take some risks with language.

## A Final Thought

Finding the words in the word search may take some students a little more time than others. There is no need to pressure students; instead allow them to create sentences with words as they find them. It is more important that they practice using the words in sentences.

# Wondrous Words

## What Is It?

Language can be a lot of fun for learners of all ages. Words are all around students every day. They hear words at home, in the community, through media, at school, and among friends and family. Wondrous Words celebrates words and language and is a way for students to share words with one another.

## How to Do It

1. Post chart paper with *Wondrous Words* written in the middle.

2. Provide each student with a sticky note. Ask students to write their favorite word on the sticky note. It can be any word they want to share.

3. Students read their words to their partners. Each student will then share their word orally with the entire class and place their sticky note on the chart paper.

## Implementation Ideas

- Once all the words are placed on the chart paper, ask students to help you think of categories for the words. Categories could include parts of speech such as nouns, adjectives, and verbs, or words could be sorted by content-area connections.

- Ask students to find partners and work together to find a way their words are connected. Have them share a sentence using both words.

- Have students think of their favorite vocabulary word within a content-area unit.

## Accommodations for Newcomers

- Provide a scaffold such as giving students a list of initial letters to spur their thinking.

- Use categories such as favorite food words or favorite action words, and ask students to share their lists orally before writing them down.

- Let students share their favorite words from their heritage language and have them offer a translation and explanation to the class.

## A Final Thought

The Wondrous Words chart captures a range of meaningful words that students contribute. They get excited about learning new words from their classmates. This activity is open-ended. In some cases, students select a word from their heritage language. This is acceptable because the activity is about celebrating words, and students can learn from one another.

# Imagine It

## What Is It?

Imagine It is a challenging activity because it relies on strong listening skills, but it is also fun because students get to draw what they hear.

## How to Do It

1. Select a picture to describe, but do not show it to the class. Think aloud as you write a description of the image. Use simple sentences that provide rich sensory descriptions.

2. Read the description to the class and ask them to just listen first. Then read it slowly and ask the class to draw what they hear.

3. Read the description once more while students check their drawings. Then have the students reveal their drawings to one another.

4. Reveal the picture that you were describing. Determine which students' drawings were closest to the actual picture. Ask students to explain which descriptive words helped them know what to draw. Below is an example of this activity.

### Imagine!

Draw what you hear:

The trees stood in a dark and eerie forest. Brown, sturdy trunks peered through the fog. The leaves of the trees drooped down on all sides while sap oozed from their trunks. The glow of the sun rising revealed their beauty.

## Implementation Ideas

- Have students work with partners. One student describes the image while the other student tries to draw what their partner described.

- Use two images; provide each partner an image to describe while their partner draws.

- After students have drawn an image, have them ask a partner to imagine something new to add to the picture. The partner describes what they imagine while the student adds to the picture.

- Ask students to describe a narrative story where this image would be the setting.

## Accommodations for Newcomers

- Provide word banks of adjectives and description words.

- Ask students to use verbs that describe actions as well as adjectives that describe features.

- Use graphic novels to model how to use text features, shapes, and fonts to portray movement, feelings, and sequences.

- Include emotion words to elicit a sense of tone.

## A Final Thought

This activity could be easily gamified by timing students as they listen for key elements and draw quickly. Since students' artistic abilities vary, keep the activity light and amusing so students feel safe expressing their ideas. This underscores the importance of a positive classroom culture and safe environment, as addressed in chapter 3.

# Blooming Reflection

## What Is It?

Using language can be intimidating for students because they must take risks knowing they will make mistakes in front of others. This activity helps build a supportive classroom environment by helping students find connections with one another and feel bonded through experiences and aspirations.

## How to Do It

1. Provide the Blooming Reflection template (see below). Tell students that they will use it to guide a conversation.

2. Explain the definition of a symbol as something that represents an idea. In this case, explain that the image of the bud represents promise, so students should think about something they are hopeful about or looking forward to.

3. The image of the thorns represents challenge, so students should consider something they are going through that is difficult or challenging.

4. Tell students that the image of the rose represents something they are proud of or something positive in their lives.

5. Ask students to consider a response for each part of the Blooming Reflection image. Have them take turns sharing their thoughts with partners or in small groups.

## Blooming Reflection

**rose**—something positive right now

**thorn**—one challenging or hard thing right now

**bud**—something you are looking forward to or are hopeful about

## Implementation Ideas

- Listen in as students share their reflections. There may be someone in the class who has had a similar experience and could provide mentorship or peer support. Consider asking students to find partners who might be able to offer some advice.

- Use this activity as part of a unit of instruction by asking students what they are hopeful about before the unit, what they are finding challenging during the unit, and what they learned or were successful with after the unit.

## Accommodations for Newcomers

- Consider that some students may have experienced trauma as newcomers. It may be difficult for them to articulate something positive. Let students know the positive thing could be as simple as a sunny day or sitting next to a friend.

- Encourage students to elaborate on a challenge they are facing by guiding them to consider ways they could address the challenge, and where they could go for help if necessary. Post resources so students know help is readily available.

- Younger students may rely on the images to spark their discussion. Remind them of what each image represents as they share orally.

- Do this activity periodically and then ask students to reflect on the past and congratulate themselves for the challenges they have overcome. Ask them to compose a letter (written or oral) to their past selves explaining how they were able to face their challenges.

## A Final Thought

When students share a reflection, they may choose to share in a heritage language. It does not take away from the real intent of the activity, which is to build community. The stronger the sense of community, the greater the likelihood that students will take risks with language.

## Language Output Strategies
# How Do You Feel?

## What Is It?

How Do You Feel? taps into students' social-emotional learning and helps build a class community. It is a quick check-in and a great way to start the day. This activity serves the purpose of getting students to use language to share how they are feeling. When students share their emotional state, you have a better idea how to approach them throughout the day. If it is a good day, you know you can push a little more, and if it is a tough day, you may wish to step back a bit. Sample images that can be used for the strategy are shown below.

## How to Do It

1. Introduce a set of emojis or other images that represent different feelings. Explain what each image represents, and ask students to describe the images in their own words.

2. Tell students that each day you will check in to see how they are feeling. Students can select one image that represents their current state of mind.

3. Ask students to share with a partner how they are feeling today, and why they chose the emoji or picture. Students may also write their responses in a daily journal.

Sample *How Do You Feel?* emojis

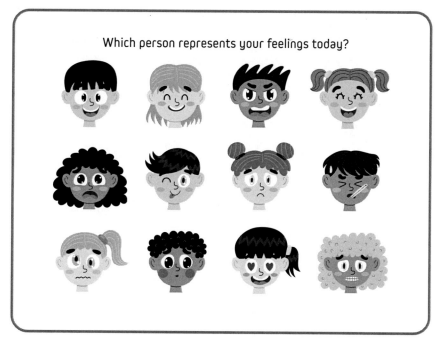

Using other images

## Implementation Ideas

- Ask students to use this activity for a character they are reading about, or for a historical figure. Have them record any changes that person underwent, and explain why their feelings changed over time.

- Laminate pictures of emojis or other emotion images and create a wall where students may post their feelings daily if they wish.

- Have students use images to represent their feelings about content they are studying; have them identify if their feelings change as they learn more about the content.

## Accommodations for Newcomers

- Have students take turns each day selecting images to use from different categories, such as superheroes, ice-cream flavors, or even different types of cars or shoes. This provides students with voice and choice, and fosters creative explanations of the relationship between an image and their feelings.

- Allow students to include words from their heritage language in their explanations.

- As a scaffold, provide an emotions word wall with translations.

## A Final Thought

For any of the language output activities, the more you know about how students are feeling, the better you can determine how to approach their learning. This strategy simply asks students to share the word, draw the emoji, or hold up the number that represents how they are feeling.

## Summary

The strategies described in this chapter give students a chance to practice a variety of thinking skills, including *identify, describe, explain, compare, give an opinion, retell, sequence, predict, relate, prove with evidence, infer, interpret, report, express emotions, check predictions*, and *identify cause and effect*. As students practice these skills, they are also developing a range of language functions. The thinking processes that students practice are a great way to develop common underlying proficiencies. Jim Cummins (1981b) showed in his research that cognitive skills and concepts learned in a language transfer across languages. Sometimes newcomers engage with the activities at first in their heritage language. This can serve as an initial rehearsal before they take risks with English. Newcomers can practice the thinking processes in any language. As their English language develops, they will begin to express their thinking in English.

There are many strategies that can be used to guide students' oral and written language development. We chose to focus on strategies that are engaging and quick for consistent daily use. They are a great way for students to practice, daily, how language is used to talk and write about content and experiences. The range of cognitive skills, the use of familiar content, and the frequency of use support the development of language fluency. These are low-stakes, language-rich activities that let students have fun with language, while simultaneously serving the critical purpose of developing academic language.

## Reflection Questions

- How could you incorporate quick fluency opportunities into your daily instruction?

- How can you establish a classroom climate that would be conducive for newcomers to take risks with language?

- What opportunities do newcomers get to practice using language for a variety of purposes to build language fluency?

# Closing Thoughts

As we reflect on this book in its entirety, there are a few key ideas that we hope you take with you. First, newcomers are an incredible group of students from whom we can learn so much. They bring unique backgrounds, perspectives, and funds of knowledge. We were honored to have the opportunity to sit down with them, listen to their stories, and share those stories with you. We hope that they have inspired you to get to know more about the newcomer students at your school; not only their demographics and reasons for coming to the United States, but about their lived experiences and interests, too.

The power of their stories leads us to our next key takeaway, which is the importance of creating an environment where newcomer students, and their families, feel safe, welcome, and a sense of belonging. There are many reasons why newcomer students come to the U.S., some of which involve trauma. The need to feel safe cannot be overstated. In addition to safety, making sure our students and families feel that they are welcome and that they belong is also critical. We learned through the newcomers' stories that without addressing those needs first, learning will be next to impossible. We hope that the strategies we shared for addressing the social and emotional considerations of your newcomers as well as for engaging their families will be helpful in getting that process started.

After establishing the importance of building a foundation of trust and social and emotional support, we dedicated the second half of the book to supporting students' access to content while also focusing on their

English language development. The theory we discussed provided context for what we know about how languages are learned most effectively. We shared information about integrated and designated ELD along with steps you can take for incorporating those essential practices in your context. The stories of the newcomers themselves are woven throughout to show how theory and practice are linked. What helped newcomers the most is supported by research. Language is part of every lesson, and the more we are aware of the ways to effectively support both content and language development, the more we will set up our students for success.

Finally, let's not forget the joy of teaching and learning. The strategies we have shared with you are not only research-based, they can also be fun. We hope that you enjoy this process and find what works best for you and your students. As the newcomers we interviewed stressed, give it time; it will be worth it in the end.

What a pleasure it has been for us to engage in this work. We appreciate the time you took to read this book and engage with us. One thing is for sure: this profession is never boring. We always have something new to learn and try. Many adventures await, and we wish you all the best on your journey to support your newcomers and their families in the classroom and beyond. Have fun, and remind yourself that you ARE making a difference.

# Resources

## Language and Literacy

Babbel. babbel.com. Subscription-based app with lessons grounded in real-world conversations.

Bilingual Magazines for all Ages. colorincolorado.org/booklist/bilingual-magazines-all-ages. Bilingual (English-Spanish) magazines and Spanish-language magazines for students who are already bilingual or are learning a new language.

Colorín Colorado. "What Are BICS and CALP?" colorincolorado.org/faq/what-are-bics-and-calp.

CommonLit. commonlit.org. Free online library of high-quality texts for third- to twelfth-grade students allows teachers and families to select lessons and reading passages for students.

Duolingo. duolingo.com. Free app with minilessons in more than 30 languages.

Global Storybooks Portal. globalstorybooks.net. A free multilingual literacy resource for children and youth, with downloadable curated collections.

International Children's Digital Library. en.childrenslibrary.org. Provides access to 4,000 children's books from around the world.

NYS Statewide Language Regional Bilingual Education Resource Network. "Bilingual Glossaries and Cognates." steinhardt.nyu.edu/metrocenter/language-rbern/education/bilingual-glossaries-and-cognates. Offers bilingual glossaries and cognates that can be used as testing accommodations or for instruction for ELL and MLL students.

Poems for Everyone. colorincolorado.org/booklist/poems-everyone. This page provides information about books with poems from different cultures. Many are bilingual in English and Spanish.

Roach, Claire, and Tim Jacklich. 2018. "Starting a Heritage Language Book Club." *Edutopia*, July 20, 2018. edutopia.org/article/starting-heritage-language-book-club.

Rosetta Stone. rosettastone.com. Subscription-based app offering language lessons.

Spanish Cognates. spanishcognates.org. Provides a comprehensive list of Spanish cognates.

Storyline Online. storylineonline.net. Videos of actors reading children's books alongside creative illustrations.

Unite for Literacy. uniteforliteracy.com. Free access to appealing ebooks that celebrate children's diverse languages and cultures.

World Stories. worldstories.org.uk. Traditional tales and new short stories in multiple languages.

## Classroom Tools

Canva. canva.com. Design software with a free version; includes templates, photos, and graphics.

Diverse Holiday Calendar. seramount.com/articles/category/heritage-months. Highlights important celebrations around the world; includes a downloadable version.

ELL Lady. ell-lady.com. Teaching tips, peer coaching advice, free resources, and lesson plans.

Google My Map. support.google.com/mymaps. Create and share maps online.

Greeting Students at the Door
- "Making Connections with Greetings at the Door." *Edutopia*. youtube.com/watch?v=GVAKBnXIGxA
- "Atlanta Teacher Has Students Recite Positive Affirmations." *NowThis Kids*. youtube.com/watch?v=7Fkkh0l0Yoo
- "Teacher Has Personalized Handshakes With Every Single One of His Students." *ABC News*. youtube.com/watch?v=I0jgcyfC2r8

Piktochart. piktochart.com. Software and design tools for creating infographics, presentations, posters, and templates.

Puzzlemaker. puzzlemaker.discoveryeducation.com/word-search. Allows you to create and print customized word search, criss-cross, math puzzles and more, using your own word lists.

Visual Schedule. ell-lady.com/freeeslresources.html. Help newcomers navigate their class schedules using a visual version.

## Social and Emotional Needs and Safe Schools

American School Counselor Association. "Eliminating Racism and Bias in Schools: The School Counselor's Role." *School Counseling Standards in Practice*. schoolcounselor.org/getmedia/542b085a-7eda-48ba-906e-24cd3f08a03f/SIP-Racism-Bias.pdf

American School Counselor Association. 2019. "Support Safe and Healthy Schools for LGBTQ Students." Webinar. videos.schoolcounselor.org/support-safe-and-healthy-schools-for-lgbtq-students.

Anti-Defamation League. 2016. "11 Ways Schools Can Help Students Feel Safe in Challenging Times." adl.org/education/resources/tools-and-strategies/11-ways-schools-can-help-students-feel-safe-in-challenging.

Berger, Tom. 2020. "How to Maslow Before Bloom All Day Long." *Edutopia*, September 23, 2020. edutopia.org/article/how-maslow-bloom-all-day-long.

CASEL (Collaborative for Academic, Social, and Emotional Learning). casel.org. Resources for making social-emotional learning a part of PK-12 education.

Centers for Disease Control and Prevention. "LGBT Youth Resources." cdc.gov/lgbthealth/youth-resources.htm.

Colorín Colorado. "Social and Emotional Support for ELLs and Immigrant Students." colorincolorado.org/teaching-ells/creating-welcoming-classroom/social-emotional-support-ells-and-immigrant-students.

Colorín Colorado. 2018. "How to Support Immigrant Students and Families: Strategies for Schools and Early Childhood Programs." colorincolorado.org/immigration/guide/student.

Coursera. "Managing Emotions in Times of Uncertainty and Stress." ycei.org/yale-course-media-kit. Free course introduces the five skills for emotional intelligence to help educators better manage their emotions and support their students.

Cowan, Katherine C., Kelly Vaillancourt, Eric Rossen, and Kelly Pollitt. 2013. "A Framework for Safe and Successful Schools" [Brief]. Bethesda, MD: National Association of School Psychologists. nasponline.org/schoolsafetyframework.

Desautels, Lori. 2016. "Five Ways to Help Students in Trauma." *Edutopia*, November 14, 2016. edutopia.org/article/5-ways-help-students-trauma-lori-desautels.

ELL Lady and Saddleback Educational Publishing. 2021. "Supporting High School Newcomers on the First Day and Beyond." Webinar. youtube.com/watch?v=pw90QnNi9Cc.

Ginwright, Shawn. 2018. "The Future of Healing: Shifting From Trauma Informed Care to Healing Centered Engagement." *Medium*, May 31, 2018. ginwright.medium.com/the-future-of-healing-shifting-from-trauma-informed-care-to-healing-centered-engagement-634f557ce69c.

GLSEN (Gay, Lesbian, and Straight Education Network). glsen.org. Resources and a network of students, families, educators, and education advocates working to create safe schools.

Howell, Christopher. 2020. "To Sustain the Tough Conversations, Active Listening Must Be the Norm." *Learning for Justice*, November 12, 2020. tolerance.org/magazine/to-sustain-the-tough-conversations-active-listening-must-be-the-norm.

Miller, Kathleen K., Calla R. Brown, Maura Shramko, and Maria Veronica Svetaz. 2019. "Applying Trauma-Informed Practices to the Care of Refugee and Immigrant Youth: 10 Clinical Pearls." *Children (Basel)* 6 (8): 94. ncbi.nlm.nih.gov/pmc/articles/PMC6721394.

Moutier, Christine, and Doreen S. Marshall. 2019. "Model School District Policy on Suicide Prevention: Model Language, Commentary, and Resources" (2nd ed.). afsp.org/ModelSchoolPolicy. New York: American Foundation for Suicide Prevention, American School Counselor Association, National Association of School Psychologists and The Trevor Project.

National Clearinghouse for English Language Acquisition. "Social and Emotional Supports for Newcomer Students." ncela.ed.gov/files/feature_topics/newcomers/ElevatingELs_SocialEmotionalSupportNewcomer.pdf.

National Network of State Teachers of the Year. 2018. "Discussion Guide: Courageous Conversations About Race in Schools." nnstoy.org/wp-content/uploads/2018/01/Discussion-Guide-Courageous-Conversations-about-Race-in-Schools.pdf.

Performance Health. 2022. "15 Fidget Tools (Not Toys) for Your Classroom." performancehealth.com/articles/15-fidget-tools-not-toys-for-your-classroom.

Silva, Arlene. 2004. "Culturally Competent Crisis Response." nasponline.org/resources-and-publications/resources-and-podcasts/diversity-and-social-justice/cultural-competence/culturally-competent-crisis-response. National Association of School Psychologists.

The Trevor Project. thetrevorproject.org. Information and support for LGBTQ young people 24/7, all year round.

# Welcoming Newcomers and Families

Colorín Colorado. colorincolorado.org. Bilingual site for educators and families of English language learners.

Community and Family Toolkit. 2018. tesol.org/docs/default-source/advocacy/tesol-community-and-family-toolkit.pdf. A resource from Teaching English to Speakers of Other Languages (TESOL) that is designed to help engage families in classrooms, schools, and communities.

English Learner Toolkit. ncela.ed.gov/english-learner-toolkit. Tools and resources for ensuring meaningful communication with limited English proficient parents.

Family Engagement Framework. www.cde.ca.gov/ls/pf/pf/documents/famengageframeenglish.pdf. Guidance for planning, implementing, and evaluating strategies for family engagement.

Family Toolkit. ncela.ed.gov/family-toolkit. A toolkit to help families meet their children's educational needs. Available in several languages.

Green Cards and Permanent Residence in the U.S. usa.gov/green-cards. Explains how to get a Green Card to become a permanent resident.

A Guide for Engaging ELL Families. colorincolorado.org/guide/guide-engaging-ell-families-twenty-strategies-school-leaders. Twenty strategies for school leaders.

How to Reach Out to Parents of ELLs. colorincolorado.org/article/how-reach-out-parents-ells. Tips and strategies for reaching out to parents.

Making Students and Families Feel Welcome. colorincolorado.org/immigration/guide/welcome. Ways to welcome your students and their families.

Office of Refugee Resettlement. acf.hhs.gov/orr/grant-funding/key-state-contacts. Support for refugees in your state, including key state contacts who can provide specific lists of providers in your area.

National Center for Education Statistics. nces.ed.gov/. Provides education data, tools, reports, and more.

Newcomer Tool Kit. ed.gov/about/offices/list/oela/new-comer-toolkit/ncomertoolkit.pdf. Resources for establishing partnerships with families from the U.S. Department of Education Office of English Language Acquisition.

Parent Involvement Toolkit. cde.state.co.us/sites/default/files/documents/fedprograms/dl/ti_parents_pitoolkit.pdf. A toolkit to help get parents involved in your school.

TIPS: Teachers Involve Parents in Schoolwork. cde.state.co.us/uip/tips_interactive_homework. Ready-made TIPS homework activities to increase family engagement. An example of TIPS for Literacy can be found at cde.state.co.us/uip/tips_literacy_k_3_final_manual_for_teachers_cde.

Unaccompanied Minors in School: What You Need to Know. colorincolorado.org/sites/default/files/Unaccompanied_Minors_Tip_Sheet_for_Colorin_Colorado-FINAL.pdf. A comprehensive guide.

United States Citizenship and Immigration Services. uscis.gov. Site for learning about eligibility and filing requirements; includes an online application and downloadable forms.

# References

Adichie, Chimamanda Ngozi. 2009. "The Danger of a Single Story." TEDGlobal. July 2009. www.ted.com/talks/chimamanda_ngozi_adichie_the_danger_of_a_single_story.

Anderson, Lorin W., and Krathwohl, David R. (Eds.). (2001) 2013. *A Taxonomy for Learning, Teaching, and Assessing: A Revision of Bloom's Taxonomy of Educational Objectives.* New York: Pearson.

Anderson, Susan L. 2021. My MLL Mentor. www.mymllmentor.com/freeeslresources.html.

Baker, Scott, Santoro, Lana, Chard, David, Fien, Hank, Park, Yonghan, and Otterstedt, Janet. 2013. "An Evaluation of an Explicit Read Aloud Intervention in Whole-Classroom Formats in First Grade." *The Elementary School Journal* 113 (3): 331–358.

Bandura, Albert. 1977. *Social Learning Theory*. Englewood Cliffs, NJ: Prentice Hall.

Batalova, Jeanne, and Jie Zong. 2016. "Language Diversity and English Proficiency in the United States." Migration Policy Institute. www.migrationpolicy.org/article/language -diversity-and-english-proficiency-united-states-2015.

Baugh, Ryan. 2022. "Refugees and Asylees: 2020 Annual Flow Report." dhs.gov/sites /default/files/2022-08/2022_0308_plcy_refugee_and_asylee_fy2020v2.pdf. Department of Homeland Security Office of Immigration Statistics.

Beard, Erin. 2021 "What Is Formative Assessment?" Teach. Learn. Grow. (blog). July 20, 2021. www.nwea.org/blog/2021/what-is-formative-assessment/.

Bloom, Benjamin S., and Krathwohl, David R. 1956. "Taxonomy of Educational Objectives: The Classification of Educational Goals," by a committee of college and university examiners. *Handbook I: Cognitive Domain*. New York: Longmans, Green.

Burgoon, Judee K., Valerie Manusov, and Laura K. Guerrero. 2021. *Nonverbal Communication*. 2nd edition. New York: Taylor and Francis.

California Department of Education. 2015. *English Language Arts/ English Language Development Framework for California Public Schools Kindergarten Through Grade Twelve*. Sacramento, CA: California Department of Education. www.cde.ca.gov/ci/rl/cf.

———. 2020. *Improving Education for Multilingual and English Learner Students: Research to Practice*. Sacramento, CA: California Department of Education. www.cde.ca.gov/sp/el /er/documents/mleleducation.pdf.

California County Superintendents Education Services Association (CCSESA). 2015. *English Learner Toolkit of Strategies*. Curriculum and Instruction Steering Committee (CISC), The Arts/English Language Development CISC Subcommittee and English Language Development Workgroup. ccsesa.org/english-learner-toolkit-of-strategies/.

Collier, Virginia. 1987. "Age and Rate of Acquisition of Second Language for Academic Purposes." *TESOL Quarterly* 21 (4): 617–641.

Colorín Colorado. 2018. "Making Students and Families Feel Welcome." *Colorín Colorado*. www.colorincolorado.org/immigration/guide/welcome.

———. 2019. "Basic Interpersonal Communication Skills (BICS)." *Colorín Colorado*. www.colorincolorado.org/glossary/basic-interpersonal-communication-skills-bics.

Cummins, Jim. 1980. "The Cross-Lingual Dimensions of Language Proficiency: Implications for Bilingual Education and the Optimal Age Issue." *TESOL Quarterly* 14 (2): 175–187.

———. 1981a. "Age on Arrival and Immigrant Second Language Learning in Canada: A Reassessment." *Applied Linguistics* 1: 132–149.

———. 1981b. "The Role of Primary Language Development in Promoting Educational Success for Language Minority Students." In California State Department of Education (Ed.), *Schooling and Language Minority Students: A Theoretical Framework*, 3–49. Los Angeles: Evaluation, Dissemination and Assessment Center, California State University.

———. 2000. *Language, Power and Pedagogy: Bilingual Children in the Crossfire*. Clevedon, UK: Multilingual Matters.

———. 2008. "BICS and CALP: Empirical and Theoretical Status of the Distinction." In *Encyclopedia of Language and Education*, Volume 2: Literacy, 2nd edition, edited by Brian Street and Nancy H. Hornberger, 71–83. New York: Springer Science + Business Media LLC.

Dutro, Susana, and Moran, Carrol. 2003. "Rethinking English language Instruction: An Architectural Approach." In *English Learners: Reaching the Highest Level of English Literacy*, edited by Gilbert Garcia. Newark, DE: International Reading Association.

Dweck, Carol S. 2013. *Mindset: The New Psychology of Success*. New York: Ballantine Books.

Echevarria, Jana, MaryEllen Vogt, and Deborah J. Short. 2008. *Making Content Comprehensible for English Learners: The SIOP® Model*. 3rd edition. Boston: Allyn and Bacon.

English Language Proficiency Assessments for California (ELPAC). 2022. California Department of Education, Educational Testing Service. www.elpac.org.

Epstein, Joyce L. 2016. *TIPS: Teachers Involve Parents in Schoolwork: Manual for Teachers*. John Hopkins University. www.cde.state.co.us/uip/tips_literacy_k_3_final_manual_for _teachers_cde.

Epstein, Joyce L., and Associates. 2019. *School, Family, and Community Partnerships: Your Handbook for Action*. 4th edition. Thousand Oaks, CA: Corwin.

Epstein, Joyce L., and Frances L. Van Voorhis. 2001. "More than Minutes: Teachers' Roles in Designing Homework." *Educational Psychologist* 36: 181–194.

——. 2012. "The Changing Debate: From Assigning Homework to Designing Homework." In *Contemporary Debates in Child Development and Education*, edited by Sebastian Suggate and Elaine Reese, 263–273. London: Routledge.

Esterline, Cecilia, and Jeanne Batalova. 2022. "Frequently Requested Statistics on Immigrants and Immigration in the United States." Migration Policy Institute. migrationpolicy.org/article/frequently-requested-statistics-immigrants-and -immigration-united-states.

Every Student Succeeds Act, 20 U.S.C. § 6301. 2015. congress.gov/114/plaws/publ95/PLAW -114publ95.pdf

Fisher, Douglas, and Nancy Frey. 2010. *Guided Instruction: How to Develop Confident and Successful Learners*. Alexandria: ASCD.

——. 2013. "Engaging the Adolescent Learner: Gradual Release of Responsibility Instructional Framework." *IRA E-ssentials*. Newark, DE: International Reading Association.

——. 2021. *Better Learning Through Structured Teaching: A Framework for the Gradual Release of Responsibility*. 3rd edition. Alexandria, VA: ASCD.

Fleming, Nora. 2019. "Why Diverse Classroom Libraries Matter." *Edutopia*. June 14, 2019. www.edutopia.org/article/why-diverse-classroom-libraries-matter.

Flynt, E. Sutton and William G. Brozo. 2008. "Content Literacy: Developing Academic Language: Got Words?" *The Reading Teacher* 61 (6): 500–502.

Freeman, Yvonne, and David Freeman. 2018. *Dual Language Essentials for Teachers and Administrators*. 2nd edition. Portsmouth, NH: Heinemann.

Gee, James Paul. 2004. *Situated Language and Learning: A Critique of Traditional Schooling*. New York: Routledge.

Genzuk, Michael. 2003. *Specially Designed Academic Instruction in English (SDAIE) for Language Minority Students*. Los Angeles: Center for Multicultural and Multilingual Research, University of Southern California.

Gonzalez, Norma, Luis C. Moll, and Cathy Amanti (Eds.). 2005. *Funds of Knowledge: Theorizing Practices in Households, Communities, and Classrooms*. New York: Lawrence Erlbaum Associates.

Hammond, Zaretta. 2015. *Culturally Responsive Teaching and the Brain: Promoting Authentic Engagement and Rigor Among Culturally and Linguistically Diverse Students*. Thousand Oaks, CA: Corwin.

Kaplan, Emily. 2020. "What Isolation Does to Undocumented Immigrants." *The Atlantic*, May 27, 2020. www.theatlantic.com/family/archive/2020/05/isolated-undocumented -immigrant/612130/

Kinsella, Kate, and Tonya Ward Singer. 2011. "Linguistic Scaffolds for Writing Effective Language Objectives." Unpublished workshop material.

Krashen, Stephen D. 1981. *Second Language Acquisition and Second Language Learning*. Oxford: Pergamon.

——. 1982. *Principles and Practices in Second Language Acquisition*. Oxford: Pergamon.

Krashen, Stephen D., and Tracey D. Terrell. 1983. *The Natural Approach: Language Acquisition in the Classroom*. Alemany: San Francisco.

Levinson, Amanda. 2011. "Unaccompanied Immigrant Children: A Growing Phenomenon with Few Easy Solutions." Migration Policy Institute. www.migrationpolicy.org/article /unaccompanied-immigrant-children-growing-phenomenon-few-easy-solutions/

Lundy-Ponce, Giselle. 2010. "Migrant Students: What We Need to Know to Help Them Succeed." Colorín Colorado. www.colorincolorado.org/article/migrant-students-what -we-need-know-help-them-succeed.

Maslow, Abraham H. 1943. "A Theory of Human Motivation." *Psychological Review* 50 (4): 370–96.

Merriam-Webster. 2022a. Advocacy. www.merriam-webster.com/dictionary/advocacy.

——. 2022b. Immigrant. www.merriam-webster.com/dictionary/immigrant.

——. 2022c. Migrant. www.merriam-webster.com/dictionary/migrant.

Mora-Flores, Eugenia. 2018. *Integrated English Language Development: Supporting English Learners Across the Curriculum*. Huntington Beach, CA: Shell.

——. 2020. "Distance Learning Guide." California Teachers Association.

National Center for Education Statistics. 2021. "Table 204.27: English Language Learner (ELL) Students Enrolled in Public Elementary and Secondary Schools, by Home Language, Grade and Selected Student Characteristics: Selected Years, 2008 -09 through Fall 2019." Digest of Education Statistics. Washington DC: Institute of Education Sciences, U.S. Department of Education. nces.ed.gov/programs/digest/d21 /tables/dt21_204.27.asp.

Office of Refugee Resettlement. (ORR). 2021a. "About the Program." April 29, 2021. www .acf.hhs.gov/orr/programs/ucs/about.

——. 2021b. "Facts and Data." December 20, 2021. www.acf.hhs.gov/orr/about/ucs/facts -and-data.

——. 2022. "Key State Contacts." June 6, 2022. www.acf.hhs.gov/orr/grant-funding/key -state-contacts.

Olsen, Laurie. 2014. *Meeting the Unique Needs of Long-Term English Language Learners: A Guide for Educators*. Washington, DC: National Education Association.

Pearson, P. D., and G. Gallagher. 1983. "The Gradual Release of Responsibility Model of Instruction." *Contemporary Educational Psychology* 8: 112–123.

Peregoy, Suzanne, and Owen Boyle. 2017. *Reading, Writing, and Learning in ESL: A Resource Book for Teaching K-12 English Learners.* 7th edition. Boston, MA: Pearson.

Riches, Caroline, and Fred Genesee. 2006. "Crosslinguistic and Crossmodal Issues." In *Educating English Language Learners: A Synthesis of Research Evidence*, edited by Fred Genesee and Kathryn Lindholm Leary, 64–108. Cambridge, UK: Cambridge University Press.

Saunders, William, Claude Goldenberg, Claude, and David Marcelletti. 2013. "English Language Development: Guidelines for Instruction." *American Educator* 37 (2): 13–25, 38–39.

Swain, Merrill. 1985. "Communicative Competence: Some Roles of Comprehensible Input and Comprehensible Output in its Development." In *Input in Second Language Acquisition*, edited by S. Gass and C. Madden, 235–253. Rowley, MA.: Newbury House.

United Nations High Commissioner for Refugees (UNHCR). 2022. *Global Trends: Forced Displacement in 2021.* Copenhagen: UNHCR. www.unhcr.org/en-us/globaltrends.html.

United States Census Bureau. 2021. "Selected Characteristics of the Foreign-born Population by Period of Entry into the United States." Accessed March 24, 2022. data.census.gov/cedsci/table?q=foreign%20born%20school&tid=ACSST1Y2019. S0502&hidePreview=true.

United States Citizenship and Immigration Services (USCIS). 2020. "Green Card Eligibility Categories." Accessed March 24, 2022. www.uscis.gov/green-card/green-card -eligibility-categories.

United States Department of Education, Office of English Language Acquisition (OELA). 2016. *Newcomer Tool Kit.* Washington, DC: OELA. www2.ed.gov/about/offices/list/oela/newcomers-toolkit/index.html.

———. 2017. *English Learner Tool Kit for State and Local Education Agencies.* Washington, DC: OELA. ncela.ed.gov/files/english_learner_toolkit/OELA_2017_ELsToolkit_508C.pdf.

United States Department of Homeland Security (DHS). 2020. *Refugees and Asylees.* Updated January 9, 2020. www.dhs.gov/immigration-statistics/refugees-asylees.

Valenzuela, Angela. 1999. *Subtractive Schooling: U.S.-Mexican Youth and the Politics of Caring.* Albany, NY: State University of New York Press.

Van Voorhis, Frances L. 2003. Interactive Homework in Middle School: Effects on Family Involvement and Students' Science Achievement." *Journal of Educational Research* 96: 323–339.

———. 2011a. "Adding Families to the Homework Equation: A Longitudinal Study of Family Involvement and Mathematics Achievement." *Education and Urban Society* 43: 313–338.

———. 2011b. "Costs and Benefits of Family Involvement in Homework." *Journal of Advanced Academics* 22: 220–249.

Vygotsky, Lev S. 1978. *Mind in Society: The Development of Higher Psychological Processes.* Cambridge, MA: Harvard University Press.

Webb, Norman L. 2002. *Depth-of-Knowledge Levels for Four Content Areas.* Unpublished paper.

WIDA. 2007. *The WIDA English Language Proficiency Standards, PreKindergarten through Grade 12.* Board of Regents of the University of Wisconsin System.

Wilson, Leslie O. 2001. "Bloom's Taxonomy Revised." The Second Principle. thesecondprinciple.com.

Yale Center for Emotional Intelligence. 2022. "About Us." medicine.yale.edu/childstudy/services/community-and-schools-programs/center-for-emotional-intelligence/about/.

Zak, Danilo. 2021. "Explainer: Emergency Shelters and Facilities Housing Unaccompanied Children." *National Immigration Forum.* immigrationforum.org/article/explainer-emergency-shelters-and-facilities-housing-unaccompanied-children/.

Zwiers, Jeff. (2008) 2014. *Building Academic Language: Essential Practices for Content Classrooms, Grades 5-12.* San Francisco, CA: Jossey-Bass.

# Glossary

**affective filter**—a metaphor that describes a learner's attitudes that affect language learning. Negative emotions such as anxiety, fear, or embarrassment can hinder language learning.

**asset-based environment**—an instructional approach that focuses on strengths, viewing diversity of thought, culture, and traits as positive assets; a classroom in which teachers and students are valued for what they bring rather than being characterized by what they may need to work on or what they lack

**asylum seeker/asylee**—a person who meets the same criteria as a refugee (fleeing danger, persecution, or violence in their country of origin), but who is already in the United States or is seeking admission at a port of entry (USDHS 2020). If/when asylum seekers are granted asylum, they are referred to as asylees.

**asynchronous learning**—learning tasks, activities, and experiences that students engage in outside of regularly scheduled class time

**Basic Interpersonal Communicative Skills (BICS)**—language skills needed for everyday social interactions such as face-to-face conversations with friends, texting, and speaking on the phone

**cognates**—words that have the same linguistic derivation (from the same original word or root) in two or more languages; for example, *chocolate* in English = *chocolate* in Spanish = *chocolat* in French; another example—English *is*, German *ist*, and Latin *est* are from Indo-European *esti*

**Cognitive Academic Language Proficiency (CALP)**—proficiency in academic language or language used in the classroom in the various content areas

**deconstructed objective**—an objective that has been broken down into parts so that each part can be addressed

**ELPAC**—the English Language Proficiency Assessments for California (ELPAC) is (at the time of this writing) the required test for English language proficiency (ELP) that must be given to students in California whose primary language is a language other than English.

**emojis**—pictographs of faces, objects, or symbols

**formative assessment**—a process to capture levels of knowledge and skill along the learning journey so teachers and students can make small, immediate, impactful decisions to support well-being, learning-goal achievement, and self-efficacy (Beard 2021)

**gradual release of responsibility**—a method of instruction in which the cognitive load shifts slowly and purposefully from teacher-as-model, to joint responsibility, to independent practice and application by the learner (Pearson and Gallagher 1983)

**guided instruction**— an instructional practice in which the teacher uses appropriate scaffolds while students are engaged in productive group work with their peers (Fisher and Frey 2010)

**heritage language**—also known as *first language* or *L1*, this is a language spoken in the home that is different from the dominant language used in academic or social settings

**heritage speakers**—students who are typically born in the United States and who speak a language other than English at home

**immigrant**—a person who comes to a country to live in it permanently

**immigrant (documented)**—a resident of the United States who has obtained their green card, which allows them to live and work permanently in the country

**immigrant (undocumented)**—a resident of the United States who has not yet obtained their green card

**international adoptee**—children who have been adopted from countries outside of the U.S.

**language targets**—language objectives; statements that describe how students will use language to demonstrate their learning

**learning management system (LMS)**—software used to manage, document, and deliver classes and learning resources. Learning management systems help monitor student participation and assess student performance

**long-term English learner (LTEL)**—an English learner who has been in United States schools for six years or more without reaching levels of proficiency in English (based on assessments) in order to be reclassified (Olsen 2014).

**migrant students**—children of migrant workers who move back and forth regularly between states or countries of residence

**newcomer**—a person recently arrived in the United States from another country—usually within the last year or two (U.S. Department of Education 2016)

**reclassification**—a process in which English learners demonstrate proficiency in district and/or state language expectations and are reclassified as English proficient

**refugee**—a person who is "unable or unwilling to return to their country of origin owing to a well-founded fear of being persecuted for reasons of race, religion, nationality, membership of a particular social group, or political opinion" (U.S. Department of Homeland Security 2020). Refugee status is documented and coordinated outside of the United States prior to arrival.

**sheltered instruction**—a means for making content comprehensible for English learners while they are developing English proficiency (Echevarria, Vogt, and Short 2008)

**sponsors**—qualified parents, guardians, relatives, or other adults to whom unaccompanied children are released; parents are preferred, followed by legal guardians, and then other adult family members

**students with limited and/or interrupted formal education (SLIFE)**—students who have gaps in formal schooling or who have not had much formal schooling at all. This can be due to migration, time in refugee camps, journeys to come to the United States, and in rare cases, because they were denied or prohibited formal access to education in their country of origin.

**transferable skills**—skills developed in one learning situation that can be transferred to another

**typologies**—the different profiles that define English learners, based on their educational background, indicating their needs, strengths, and assets related to learning English

**unaccompanied youth/minor**—child under the age of 18 who come to the United States without their parents or legal guardians

**WIDA**—WIDA stands for World-class Instructional Design and Assessment. The name WIDA originally stood for the three states on the grant proposal: Wisconsin, Delaware, and Arkansas. Today, it represents a community of member states, territories, federal agencies, and international schools. The organization developed the WIDA English Language Proficiency Standards, most recently revised in 2020, which serves as the basis for the ACCESS for ELLs test of English Language Proficiency. In addition, WIDA provides tools and resources to support multilingual learners, families, and educators.

# Index

trust, building of, 76–79

typologies, 4, 252

## U

unaccompanied minors/youth

    criteria for, 18

    defined, 17, 252

    social-emotional needs of, 19

    top countries of origin of, 17

    use of term, 13

undocumented immigrants, 13–14, 251

universities, as resource for newcomer families, 111

U.S. Census Bureau, on newcomer demographics, 10

U.S. Department of Education, Newcomer Tool Kit, 158

U.S. Department of Homeland Security, on newcomer demographics, 10

U.S. Department of State, on newcomer demographics, 10

## V

Valenzuela, Angela, 14

videos, student-created, 107

visual schedule, as part of newcomer kit, 91

Vogt, MaryEllen, 167

Vygotsky, Lev, 131, 179

## W

Webb, Norman L., 200

Where in the World? as language output strategy, 221–222

Which Three Do You See? as language output strategy, 223–224

"windows," use of in helping students feel they belong, 84

Wondrous Words, as language output strategy, 225–226

World-class Instructional Design and Assessment (WIDA), 10, 124, 252

*The World: A Traveler's Guide to the Planet* (Lonely Planet), 90

## Y

"yet," adding of in stories, 31–32

*Your Name Is a Song* (Thompkins-Bigelow), 86

YouTube, 171

## Z

Zone of Proximal Development (ZPD), 131–132, 179